D1356284

THE HEART OF SCOTLAND

A UNIFORM COMPANION VOLUME

THE FACE OF SCOTLAND

By HARRY BATSFORD *&* CHARLES FRY

With a Foreword by John Buchan, and 140 Illustrations. Demy 8vo. Cloth, lettered. 7*s.* 6*d.* net.

". . . The work has been very well done."

The Prime Minister

". . . A book which describes the beauties of Scotland with enthusiasm and understanding, and also with knowledge and sobriety. . . . Some of the finest specimens of the photographic art that I have seen."

John Buchan

". . . Nobody who delights in Scottish scenery can afford to deny himself this collection of photographs, the most representative I know in a book published at so low a price."

Compton Mackenzie

". . . It is the most honest book on Scottish scenery that could come your way. The text is the ideal setting of the one hundred and more photographs that are the book's glory. All are perfect in technique, and convey with a kind of nostalgic charm the rare clarity of the Highland air."

The Morning Post

". . . About as beautiful as Scotland itself."

The Edinburgh Citizen

Published by

B. T. BATSFORD LTD

15 North Audley Street, London, W. 1

1 CASTLEBAY, BARRA, OUTER HEBRIDES

From a Drawing by Keith Henderson

THE HEART OF SCOTLAND

By

GEORGE BLAKE

With a foreword by
ERIC LINKLATER

Illustrated from drawings by
BRIAN COOK
and from photographs

LONDON
B. T. BATSFORD LTD
15 NORTH AUDLEY STREET, W.1

FOR

HUGH WALPOLE

First Published, September 1934

MADE AND PRINTED IN GREAT BRITAIN
FOR THE PUBLISHERS, B. T. BATSFORD LTD., LONDON
TEXT BY UNWIN BROTHERS LTD., WOKING
PLATES BY THE DARIEN PRESS, EDINBURGH

FOREWORD

By ERIC LINKLATER

To find the mind's construction in the face is often a pretty exercise in ingenuity. To seek the Scottish mind's construction in Scotland's face is sometimes an exercise in piety, sometimes in pathology: piety if you confine your examination to the romantic forehead of the Highlands and the pastoral complexion of the Lowlands, pathology if you see only municipal architecture and the industrial belt. You should look at both: on the one hand beauty in abundance, on the other scar-tissue in superfluity. Then you may feel that some evil spirit has said to Scotland,

> Could I come near your beauty with my nails,
> I'd set my ten commandments in your face.

(Five of the ten commandments were the Reformation, which confused beauty and happiness with sin; and the other five were the Industrial Revolution, which identified quick profits with virtue.) Now an evil spirit is usually born at home, though it may be conditioned from abroad, and most of Scotland's mutilation is self-mutilation. It is necessary, therefore, to consider the nature of that spirit, and this cannot be done solely by examination of mountains and slag-heaps, of the sea-lochs and double tenements: you will have to inquire into the constitution of the Scottish people and read their history; and if you want to save yourself trouble you will hire an expert investigator. But do not go farther in your search for one. Here, for the sum of seven shillings and sixpence, is an admirable consultant: Mr. George Blake.

I admit that I began to read this book with some trepidation, because I value Mr. Blake's friendship, and, for all I knew, he might have diagnosed as Scotland's heart what I prefer to think of as her spleen; but I read on with growing confidence, and I finished it with complete satisfaction. His stethoscope has not betrayed him, and I believe that he knows the organism of Scotland as well as any man now living. He has, too, an excellent bedside manner, for his own feelings, which are not without passion, are always kept under control.

He has insight: consider his assertion that the Lowland working classes "have the sense of all but aesthetic values," and compare it with a complementary statement that "the dullness of Scottish architecture is in direct reaction to the ornamentation usually associated with Rome." He has the courage to be blunt and the grace to be calm. On one page he roundly says, in reference to Scottish drunkenness, that "living conditions almost anywhere in the industrial belt are quite enough to drive any man to drink"; and in another place he glances at the Aberdonian *hamartia* and makes the placid comment, "the people have the sense of mundane values highly developed." He can turn his stethoscope on Scotland's visitors and perceive that "the country has come to be regarded more as a picturesque playground than as an economic and social reality"; then, auscultating Scotland again, the Scot himself is discovered as unwilling to face reality, and for medicine he is reminded that "the memory of Bonnie Prince Charlie has no bearing on Bellshill, and the loveliness of Morar does not compensate for the subsidised pauperisation of the crofters."

But I must deny myself more quotations, though in justice both to Mr. Blake and to Scotland I ought to mention his insistence on the survival of a quality that has characterised Scotsmen throughout recorded time: and that is vigour. It is an invaluable quality, but sometimes an uncomfortable one, for it will, on occasion, explode into that Caledonian fury which is more useful for demolition than construction. But I need not go into that. It is Mr. Blake's duty, not mine, to explain his native fury and his native kindliness, his stern common sense and his fondness for singing "that alien and intolerable song, *My Ain Folk*"; and these and many other problems he has solved with great skill and perception.

Why he asked me to write a Foreword for a book as good as this I cannot think: it is first-rate wine and it needs no bush. But my reason for agreeing to write one is clear enough: I flatter myself by associating myself with so much wisdom. If the book has the success it deserves it will have a large success: it will be invaluable to the English traveller, and to know what Mr. Blake knows—about his own country, at any rate—is essential to every self-respecting Scot.

ERIC LINKLATER

ORKNEY, *August* 1934

LIST OF ILLUSTRATIONS

LIST OF DRAWINGS BY BRIAN COOK

AUTHOR'S NOTE

This study of Scotland as it is to-day is very much more the testimony of an individual than a thesis based tidily on facts and figures. Where such drab entities have had to be quoted in illustration of a point, the source is duly implied in the text.

Otherwise I have but to acknowledge the kindness of Mr. Eric Linklater in lending the powerful approval of his pen to this essay on our native country; the brilliance of the photographers, who have so splendidly used the rich material it provides; and the energy of Mr. Charles Fry, of Messrs. Batsford, who so quickly and sympathetically (as will be seen in his arrangement of these lovely illustrations) grasped the point that, as between the Face and the Heart of Scotland, there are many queer differences.

G. B.

GLASGOW
September 1934

CONTENTS

2 IN THE PASS OF LENY, PERTHSHIRE

3 THE HISTORIC HEART OF SCOTLAND: Edinburgh Castle from the Air

THE HEART OF SCOTLAND

CHAPTER I

BY WAY OF INTRODUCTION

"The 'Face of Scotland' is not the heart of Scotland, but, if properly discerned, it is a clue to it. Much of the idiom of the national history, character and literature can be traced to the landscape."

Thus Mr. John Buchan in his Foreword to the volume of which this is the sequel and the companion. The generalisation is a fair one, but, as nobody knows better than Mr. Buchan himself, one subject to all sorts of qualifications. It was not the lure of the bright hills of Knapdale, with the evening sun upon them, that brought the Scots from Ireland to found their kingdom of Dalriada; nor was it so much what was on the ground as what lay beneath it that produced the biggest factor in the making of modern Scotland, the industrial development of the nineteenth century. But we can be grateful to Mr. Buchan for an idea, a title and a word; so be it we remember that while the face of Scotland is fair and an increasingly important part of her fortune, the country is not wholly understood in terms of landscape alone. The loveliness of so much of it is apt, indeed, to mislead us past the truth about Scotland. For if it is a clue to the Scottish spirit, it is no more than a clue, and we shall find richer veins in history, dynastic and economic and theological, in geology and ethnology, even in the weather itself.

This book will not seek to delve deeply, if at all, into these drab elements behind the Scottish ethos. Its business is to show what that is and how it works to-day. Its concern is mainly with the people and how they live, are apt to think and feel, how they fare in the daily round, suffer, laugh, pray, hate and hope—all as conditioned by the circumstances in which it has pleased God to call them. We seek, in short, to discover what Mr. Buchan excellently calls "the idiom" of the national life.

And there is almost a begging of the question at once! Shall we admit the Scots to be a people apart, racially and spiritually so compact as to be utterly distinct and different from the English? That very question has taken on a political significance during the last few years, and with issues of the kind we have no concern here. Happily, history is there to clear our minds. A Scottish kingdom survived until within the negligible period of some four hundred years ago. It is little more than two hundred years since Scotland had her own Parliament, the Estates. She has still her own Church, her own code of law, and the length of the Borders from Berwick to Sark Bridge has hardly been dried of the blood of ancient wars, shed in that clash of nationality which has its curious, and sometimes disturbing, echo in the frenzies of the crowds at an international football match. Indeed, the distinction exists, and if we shall encounter many superficial similarities between the life of Scotland and that of provincial England, we shall also see that the tempers of the peoples are vastly different, and that, while large sections of each may live in comparable conditions, their comportment under these conditions is not at all the same.

This difference, this almost tangible sense of alienation as between near neighbours, must have affected everybody who has crossed the Border—as if that boundary, so lacking in spectacular quality at its western end at least, were a frontier complete with sentries and flags and customs-posts. Sentiment, of course, plays a huge part in imparting the feeling of adventure to such a crossing, and racial memory plays its part also, but it is surprising to the sensitive traveller how the mood, the temper, the attitude of people, living perhaps only ten miles apart and being in the ethnologist's sense members of precisely the same race, do quite recognisably differ

4 THE SOUTHERN UPLANDS: Gentle Tweed at Manor Bridge, near Peebles

5, 6 PASTORALS: (*above*) a Caithness Farm with Flagstone Fencing, and (*below*) Grazing in Angus

according to the side of the Tweed on which they happen to dwell. There are fusions, to be sure. There is one house just on the English side of Sark Bridge, of which the people must be as much in Scotland as in England. (Probably one would find them more self-consciously English than any Cockney group!) But from Ecclefechan to Carlisle is only twenty minutes in a modern car, and yet these towns are far-sundered as if by a wide and deep sea. Their very names shriek of the jostling of races and traditions.

It is entirely a matter of tradition, of national tradition, manifesting itself in habits imposed by law and custom. And just wherein the Scottish tradition is unique is precisely the subject of research in these pages.

But even when we reach that point of agreement, we are far from emerging from the wood. It is doubtful if any other country so small as Scotland can show such a large and dramatic range of racial variations in its population. It becomes a sane man to tread warily where scientific gentlemen treat each other with scant courtesy, but we may wonder how anything homogeneous could have been fashioned out of the early Picts—whoever they may have been—the Britons of Strathclyde, the invading Angles of the Lothians, and the invading Scots of Dalriada. We may well pause to brood on the romantic fact that the family name of Galbraith, common in the southern Hebrides, is good enough Gaelic for "British stranger." If we discount entirely the pretty legend of Spanish blood, from survivors of the Armada, in the Western Isles, we have to reckon with a strong Scandinavian element in those parts and up about Caithness and the Moray Firth. We have also to realise that it is not so long ago since Gaelic was spoken in Fife, in Ayr and in Galloway. Add to all that the confusion caused by the intense concentration of the population in the valley of Forth and Clyde as a consequence of the Industrial Revolution, and we may doubt if the identification of a uniquely typical Scot is within the bounds of possibility. As between Col Macdonald, Gaelic-speaking crofter of Knoydart, and Jock Shaw, riveter in Clydebank, what conceivable bond can be discerned other than the purely political? And that is to ignore the swarming Irish of the Glasgow area as a species of unregistered aliens.

It is simply necessary for practical purposes to take the conventional view of Scotland as consisting of two regions, differently peopled, the Highlands and the Lowlands. To take Scotland thus in black and white is neither good history nor good geography. There would be reason in regarding the industrial belt as a corridor apart or a melting-pot of all the elements in the country. But as the Lowland tradition tends to prevail in that thickly populated area (with some queer and charming exceptions that will be duly noted) the rough division is permissible and useful. Circumstances have conspired to give the Highlanders and the Lowlanders—each group so variously composed—what can be regarded as distinct identities; and if a line be drawn on a map from Elgin to Dumbarton the internal frontier is marked as clearly as may be.

Again, let us not forget that these elements are capable of infinite permutations and combinations, and that the line is, in fact, far from being a straight one. But the latter does divide Scotland accurately enough. It is a country of two races, one mainly Celtic and one mainly Teuton. It is a country of two languages, Gaelic and English. (Some would reasonably say three, for Braid Scots has its own identity and pride.) It is a country of two cultures and traditions.

Later on, we shall see how far the factors are sympathetic and how far they are apparently irreconcilable. The clash of them is indeed a contemporary Scottish problem. Some grimly foresee the triumph of the practical Lowland spirit. Some dream of a Scotland reawakened to a consciousness of its Celtic inheritance. At the moment, it is enough that the dichotomy is there and still unresolved—even if we must not thereupon conclude that the parts do not share a something which brands every manjack of both sorts as Scots pure and simple.

It would take a long time to tell how this welter of tribes became a nation and achieved an identity. The history books say that Robert the Bruce (whom one is tempted to regard as being really a somewhat unscrupulous Norman adventurer) crowned at Bannockburn the work begun centuries before and hastened most notably by the genuine native patriot, William Wallace. One might almost as well say that Scotland was created a nation by the ambition of the English. For even if the long Wars of Independence confirmed the solidarity and shape of the country as we know it to-day, there remained for centuries thereafter a distinct uneasiness as between the nominal governors, with their headquarters in Stirling or Edinburgh, and the Highlanders with their own tribal organisation of clans, their own clan feuds, and their pretty custom of invading the fat Lowlands for cattle and provender generally.

It is the paradox of Scottish history that there was no true internal peace until the Highlands were mercilessly emasculated in revenge for the parts played by some of the clans in the Jacobite risings of 1715 and 1745. It might be said that the Highlander has never recovered from that humiliation. But it is well worth noting that these rebellions took place long after the Union of the Crowns and even after the more effective Union of the Parliaments. And something like Jacobitism is still cherished as more than a pretty sentimentality in many a Highland breast.

It may not have been a compact Scotland that existed when Mary of Scots came to the throne, but, however uneasy its balance, it was to pass as one nation through certain crises that, not necessarily peculiar to Scotland, inflicted on the people marks, deep and lasting, that so affected—one had almost said warped—the Scottish character that whatever differences may have existed between the Scots and the English were thereby and for ever emphasised and made permanent. It would seem on the face of it that the establishment of Scottish independence by the Bruce and the loss of it in the Union of 1707 were the fatal passages in the national history, but it is tenable that the Reformation and the Industrial Revolution are responsible for more in the character of the Scot to-day than are any considerations of race and merely dynastic history.

All Britain felt the force of the Reformation—and England made out of it the charming and characteristic compromise of Episcopalianism. When Scotland was infected, it had to be all or nothing—and the result was Calvinism unadulterated, if not a little intensified.

The difference between these results requires some explanation. We can say that life in a relatively barren land had encouraged a hard and absolute way of thinking. We know that the Scottish Reformers in their excessive zeal had not the simple motives of Henry the Eighth, but had the political grievances of an outraged democracy to fire them; so that they did not rest content, in the good imperial way, with the confiscation of the Church's money and lands, but went out to smash all the emblems of Popery—and Englishness.

> And wi' John Calvin i' their heads,
> And hammers i' their hands and spades,
> Enrag'd at idols, mass and beads,
> Dang the Cathedral down.

How curiously prophetic that, on the mainland, only the Cathedral of Glasgow survived completely unscathed the reforming enthusiasms!

The violence of that reaction is not comprehensible in English terms. It was a desperation of destruction beyond folks living in an easy land. It was the wildest, maddest, and in its way most splendid outburst of the *furor caledoniensis*. It was probably really more significant than Bannockburn.

For if the act of rebellion was ferocious, the reaction to years of unhappiness and disorder under frenchified rule was excessive. Scotland took to the severest presbyterianism, and theological hair-splitting became a national pursuit. The Roman Church became the Whore of Babylon or, in milder moments, the Scarlet Woman—varied by references to the something unspeakable "that sitteth upon seven hills." And so intense was the passion for purity, there inevitably developed a sort of competition in faith; so that the country was plunged into schism and controversy—a state from which it has not yet fully emerged. There is always a rump for every movement within Scottish Presbyterianism; and a chart, a tree, of the subdivisions of that faith at, say, the end of the eighteenth century has to be seen to be believed. In J. M. Barrie's *Auld Licht Idylls* we learn something of the intensity of denominational feeling at a relatively recent date.

Yet it must never be forgotten that theological fury in Scotland has always been, in part, political. The extremism of the early Presbyterians was always at least a little in defiance of what they called prelatical influence from the South. The Covenanting movement was really a last flicker of the ancient and now lost War of Independence. Nor should we forget that the Reformation dashed its fierce self in vain against the conservatism and remoteness of several Highland clans. Some took easily to the Reformation—notably the powerful Campbells, always shrewd in Scottish politics. But there are Macdonalds and such on the western seaboard and in the Isles whose Catholicism is of pre-Reformation vintage and serenely antedates everything else in the religious life of the country.

But when all exceptions are stated and all allowances made, the Reformation remains a supreme influence in the trend of the Scottish character as it is to-day. Too many things are counted among its legacies, but if the Scot is given to controversy, to niggling after fine shades of meaning, to literalism, to taking his pleasures sadly, or madly, and to stubbornness, much of what he is can be traced back to that enormous upheaval and the sad centuries of controversy and repression that followed it.

The Reformation—then the Revolution; and if we can understand how a very sudden onrush of industrialism would be likely to affect a grave and theologically inclined people, we shall really know most of the truth about modern Scotland, so far as the vast majority of the population is concerned.

It was about 1800 a mainly agricultural country, with some decent industries of the weaving and distilling sorts. Coal had been mined in a quiet domestic way, and here and there were black spots where men hewed and smelted iron ore. The Tobacco Lords of Glasgow were still importing the produce of Virginia and wearing, haughtily, their scarlet cloaks. Fishing was a staple, as it still is, even in difficult times; and Leith, Dundee, Aberdeen, Irvine and Greenock were ports of consequence. But it was on the whole a modest and conventional economy; and it is strange to think that it was so violently upset and developed along new lines by virtue of the discoveries and inventions of Scotsmen.

A boy in Greenock watched a kettle boiling and glimpsed the truth that made the steam engine a practical proposition. A mile or two along the road towards Glasgow a strange and interesting man got John Wood to build the *Comet*. The new wealth gleamed before the eyes of men. Scotland had the coal and iron they needed. And suddenly, as we reckon history, a belt across the middle of Scotland was reeking with smoke, and men were pouring in from the hills and pastures and glens, and from overseas, to dig their living from the earth, to scarify miles of loveliness, to make new towns and railways and canals—and slums.

The experience was not unique. We all know what it means to any country. But it meant almost everything to Scotland, a small and curiously constituted land. It

9 THE EMPTY HIGHLANDS: Ruined Cottages near Aberfoyle

10 CHILDREN AND TENEMENTS IN GLASGOW

meant the importation of cheap labour from Poland and Lithuania, and it meant a huge invasion from poverty-stricken Ireland that has given Scotland one of its chronic problems. It meant the uglification of fine old towns and the haphazard building of ugly new ones. It meant a herding, an enslavement, and a vast vulgarisation. It meant, above all, the concentration of four-fifths of the total population in a mere strip of a tiny province.

The inherited qualities did not, of course, thereupon promptly desert the Scot. You might still find the most typical of that race among the shipyard-workers of Clydeside. But it all led to a gigantic concentration, to a fusion and a reduction of the natural elements of the population to the lowest common denominator. A new factor was created when the people flocked into the valley of the Forth and Clyde, and the units of that central mass had their aboriginal Scottishness modified, whether that Scottishness was of the Lowland or of the Highland brand. New standards were created, most of them low; and Scotland, the remote land of barbarians, was exposed to alien and levelling influences. Given a wet Sunday afternoon, it would be hard for a foreigner to-day to distinguish quite clearly between the English city of Manchester and the Scottish city of Glasgow. He would perhaps, if observant, notice a little difference in the speech of the common peoples. If his temperament inclined him to exploration he might notice that while the pubs of Manchester opened at strictly regulated hours on the Sabbath, those of Glasgow did not open at all. But if the poor fellow were condemned, as most hapless strangers are, to pass the day of rest in a hotel, he might as well be in the one country as in the other.

What industrialism did to Scotland particularly will be considered later on, but we have to understand at this early stage its effect on the Scotland that lay out of sight of the bings and the smokestacks. Roughly, but essentially, it brought about a vast depopulation of the countryside. It constituted itself a magnet that could lure men and

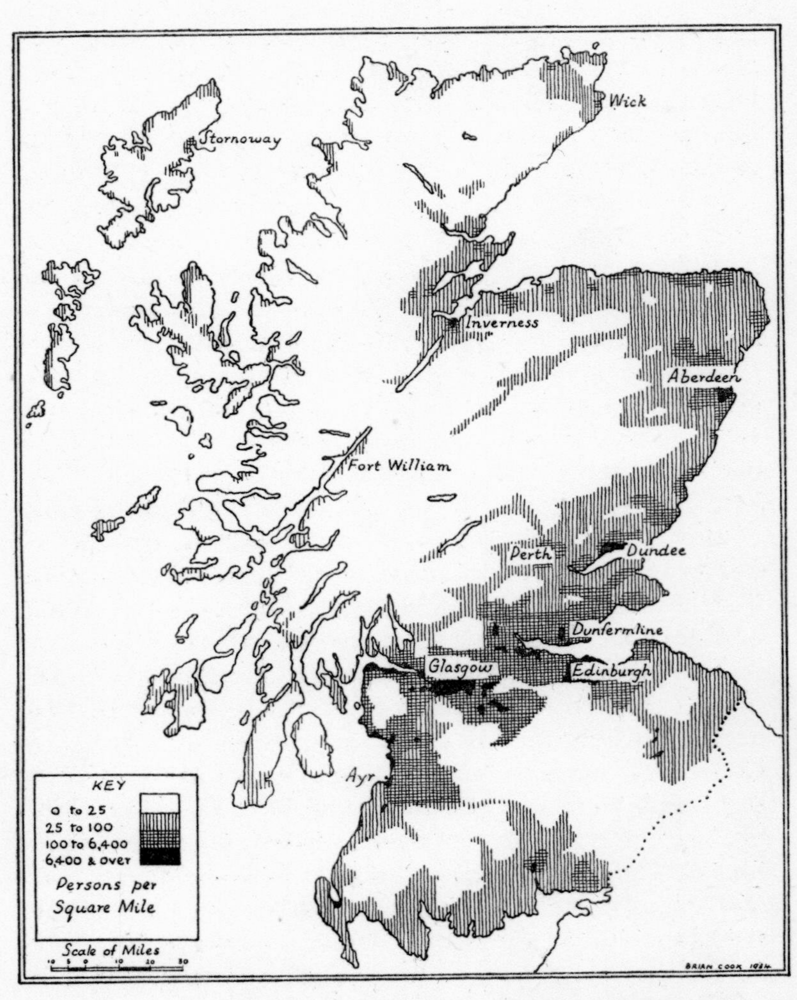

A MAP OF SCOTLAND SHOWING THE DISTRIBUTION OF POPULATION

women from where they were rather more useful in the long run to Scotland—from the soil. That lure the industrial regions still exercise. The Highlands still supply the cities with policemen, bar-tenders and domestic servants. The depopulation of the rural parts, both Highland and Lowland, proceeds at an alarming rate. It might fairly be said that modern Scotland consists of a huddle of over-populated towns and a vast expanse of abandoned land.

Fantastic changes have occurred in the brief course of a century. In his *Geographical and Statistical Account of Scotland*, published in 1819, Playfair gives the population of the County of Argyll as 85,585. The Census of 1931 returned it as 63,014. Playfair recorded the population of Greenock as being 19,402, but the last Census made it 78,948. Take into consideration the normal expectation of intercensal increase, and it is seen that a typical Lowland town has, so to speak, sucked a typical Highland county dry.

The agricultural Lowlands suffered also, but to nothing like the same extent; for the Highlander, his spirit broken by the Hanoverians, his chieftains in exile or seduced by the lure of a Court at St. James's, had to endure humiliations that affected him only. Somebody will yet tell in fiction or dispassionate history the ghastly story of the Clearances, when thousands of people, rooted to life in the glens, were evicted, in circumstances of incredible brutality, to make room for sheep and driven down to the sea, there to learn if they could a new and unfriendly way of life—or to take the ships for the Colonies that the exploiters had made ready for them. They were driven off the land, and to this day they are kept off the land.

We shall see how the Scottish brand of landlordism affects even the casual wayfarer, but we note at the moment that it has been the economic ruin of the Highlands. For the time came when the rearing of sheep ceased to promise as much return to absentee lairds as the letting of sporting rights; and grouse and deer proved even less companionable than sheep. The native man became the animal of least importance in the economy of the northern counties. Heaven knows his land was poor. But it could once support hundreds where only tens are suffered now. Again, according to Playfair, the population of Rhum was in 1819 "about 600." This somewhat notorious sporting property now supports less than a dozen natives.

The Highlander was driven out of his birthright. In many cases he fled before the writ, backed by torches for his thatched roof in cases of resistance. Otherwise, his natural life was made impossible for him. So the industrial Lowlands received him by the thousand as they still receive the surplus that an outraged territory cannot support. If he did not go in tears and to the wailing of the bagpipe down to the ships so thoughtfully provided by the men who wanted his holding for their sheep, he saved enough to take him and his family out of intolerable degradation to the lands beyond the sea. Even since the War, liners of the Canadian Pacific Company went about the Islands, collecting those useless creatures whose activities as cultivators are still regarded in certain quarters as of rather less importance than the fecundity of the red deer. Hence a good deal of the human backbone of Canada and the United States and Australasia. But it is sometimes rather bitter for a Scot to hear his people called "a great race of Empire-builders." Between 1921 and 1931 the number of Gaelic-speakers in Scotland fell from 158,779 to 136,135

Men are beginning to ask why that sort of thing should be, but we note merely the fact at the moment; and we see Scotland for what it is after those long centuries of emergency and error and heroism and exploitation. We see a people mainly Presbyterian, and hard, thorough, dour, humorous and fantastically capable of desperation withal. We see the bulk of them huddled into a short and narrow tract where minerals abound, thinly populated uplands to the south of them and mile upon mile of mountainous and superlatively lovely desolation to the north.

And now we try to understand what this complex of forces and results has made of the spirit of the Scotsman in general, and how he lives in our modern world.

REGENT ARCH, EDINBURGH

CHAPTER II

IN THE HIGHLAND PLACES

So curiously is Scotland constituted, so complex are the racial and economic forces at work within a relatively small area, it is a country studded with places that wear what one can only call an air of unexpectedness—towns, villages, views and vistas that, encountered on a journey, make a man feel that he is abroad, or that he has been absurdly carried back through centuries of time, or that the normal economy of the country has here and there turned a preposterous somersault.

Thus the town of Inveraray hits the eye of the traveller rounding the point of Strone on the road from Glasgow as something uprooted and transplanted from the Mediterranean. Those ornamental bridges that approach the town, and those high, white arches that guard it to the north, are right out of the expected tradition. (It cost a decoratively inclined Duke and his successors some £300,000 to achieve these effects at a period when that sum represented something like a million nowadays.) So also at Port Charlotte, in Islay, one seems to be visiting a deserted townlet on the Ligurian coast, so empty and echoing and white are its warehouses and streets.

Haddington and Kirkcudbright and Kelso have likewise something of that exotic, improbable quality; and so has many another Scottish town, from which, as it were, the tide of affairs has receded. The strangest effects, however, are surely created where progress, as we are pleased to call it, has taken advantage of some local condition and ventured far beyond its familiar haunts.

Thus the township of Kinlochleven, in its sombre setting of mountains, may seem to the wayfarer a piece of dark lunacy. It is not explained away by the fact that the British Aluminium Company simply took advantage of the huge reserves of water-power available in that rough northern area of Argyll. The orderly mind rejects the improbability of those belching smokestacks and geometrical rows of modern dwellings in a place designed by Nature for secret gatherings of clans and dark deeds with the claymore.

There was a time when Kinlochleven was even more of a monstrosity than it appears to-day. Often has the story been told how thousands tramped from Clydeside to seek work at the building of it, some of them to die on the mountain tracks. Up till the end of the War it was isolated—a Coatbridge lost in the Highlands—but German prisoners had cut a road along the steep hillside, and now the motorists, coming across the Moor of Rannoch over the new road from the South, and disdaining the ferry at Ballachulish, rush through it by the hundred every day. Yet familiarity could never rob the place of its grim oddity. One is glad to be through it and its blackness of smoke and shadow. There is a grim interest in the fact that a local necessity is a sun-ray clinic, 80 per cent of childish ailments there being due to lack of sunlight, shut out by the steep and unrelenting hills surrounding it.

The village of Obbe at the southern extremity of the island of Harris is an even more surprising place. The most enlightening view of it is got from the air; and from that angle it has the absurd aspect of something very up to date on Merseyside or in the Thames Valley about Slough—neat rows of sheds and warehouses, trim blocks of dwelling-houses, and cranes on the orderly quays—all on the verge of the fabled waters of the Minch, under towering, desolate mountains and in sight of Skye's fairy peaks of the Coolins.

It was, of course, the first Lord Leverhulme's dream to create here another Port Sunlight. (That is why he rechristened the place, with a monumental lack of tact, Leverburgh.) He meant well; there is no doubt of that. He aimed to bring prosperity back to the Hebrides by means of fishing fleets well equipped, cooperages of the most modern order, canneries and what not. And he failed—beaten by the Highland temperament and his own natural lack of understanding of it.

We may wonder at the precise nature of the forces that obliged a very able and active and generous man to retire from the fray. Was it mere local resentment of the Sassunach intrusion? Was it laziness, as some cruelly say? Or was it—and this is a question of immense interest and importance—the clash of a romantic and aristocratic with a realistic and acquisitive tradition?

All the elements suggested were probably behind that sensational defeat of industrialism: one of the most significant episodes in Scottish history. But we have to give the Highlander credit for a distinguished philosophy at the back of his behaviour in this strange business. It was no doubt unconscious, but it told him that the making of money is not all, and that it profits a man nothing if he gain the whole world and lose his own soul at the same time.

The case of Kinlochleven is not comparable, for that black pocket of industrialism has been mainly filled with foreigners from the beginning. Obbe remains unique and tremendously significant. It happened in Scotland—the Scotland of Big Business, of heavy industries, of the "bang went saxpence" legend; and we do not begin to understand the country until we understand why there is not a Port Sunlight in the Outer Isles to-day. The key to the problem is almost certainly in the hands of the Highlander, whom our conventions insist on regarding as either a slightly comic half-wit or an actor retired from a distinguished career on the romantic stage. It is quite certain that the queerest towns of Scotland have been created where his philosophy clashes with the brash materialism of the newer age.

Walter Scott and Robert Louis Stevenson, assisted in later days by battalions of "Scotch" comedians, have given the world at large its popular conception of the Highlander, but it must be suggested that these men of

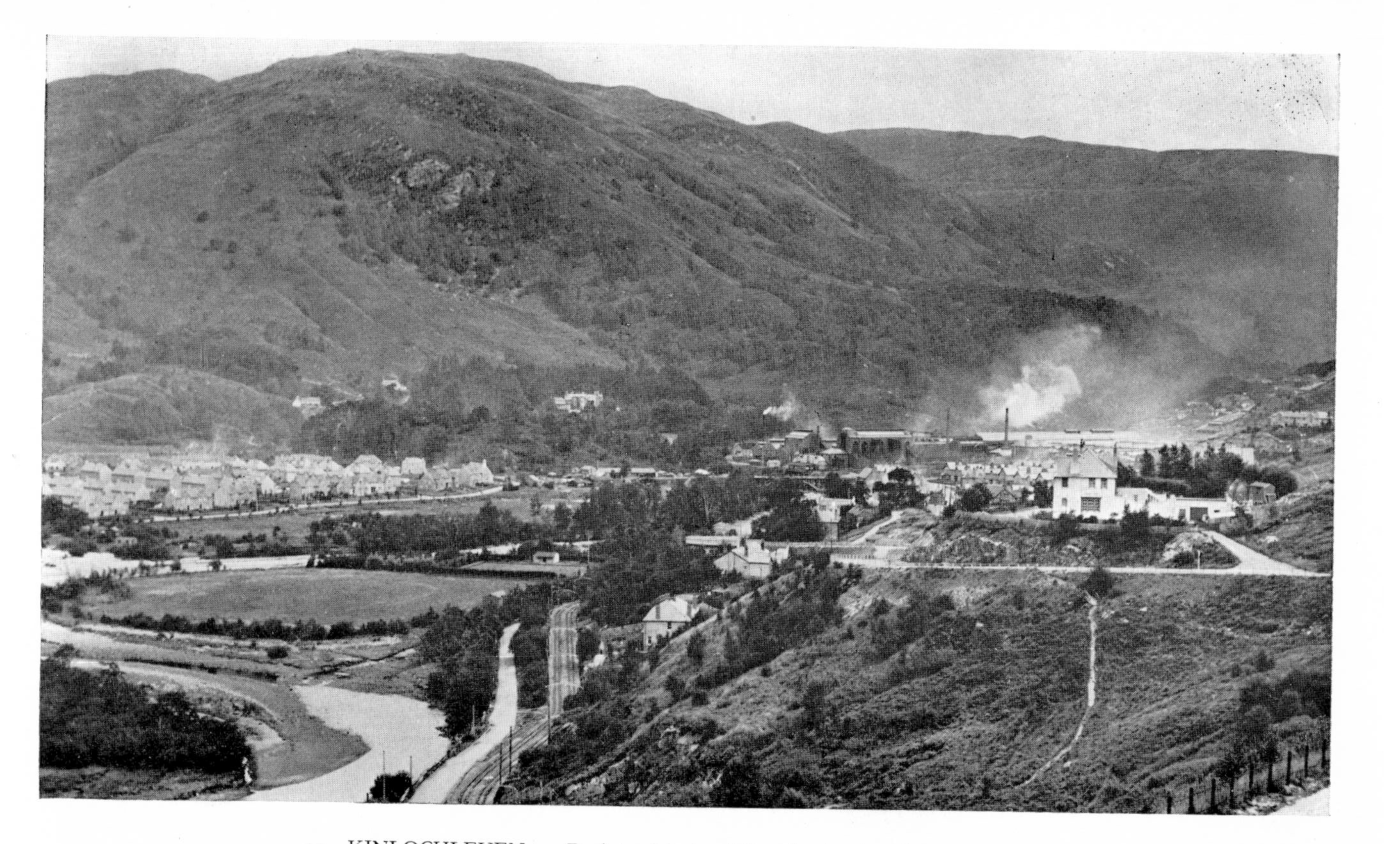

13 KINLOCHLEVEN: a Pocket of Industrialism in the Argyllshire Highlands

14 OBBE—ONCE LEVERBURGH—IN THE ISLE OF HARRIS

genius did not thoroughly know the animal they were delineating for the benefit of what would nowadays be call the library public. Scott created Dougal Cratur and a preposterous legend of a race of cunning nitwits with a lamentable, but diverting, lack of command over the English tongue—a brood of "Phairsons" eternally concerned with their "sneeshin' mulls." Stevenson fashioned his Gaels on the Lewis Waller mould, and, nearer the truth than Scott, often went far astray: as in the piping contest in Cluny's cave in *Kidnapped.* Neil Munro, when he did not follow Stevenson through the heather with a claymore at his side, gave a truer picture by right of his own pure Highland birth. In our own time Neil M. Gunn has corrected the traditional view of the man in his novels.

Yet the average traveller suffers under the illusions of the literary legend established during the nineteenth century. He is a man who is, most naturally, concerned mainly to see what delights the eye and stirs the imagination. He does not elect to pass his first Scottish week-end in Coatbridge, though it is in such places the secrets of Scotland's heart are most likely to be surprised. His concern as a holidaymaker is with the face, so that we encounter him in the Scott country, luxuriating in the moonlit glow put upon that fair region of peels and valleys and ruined abbeys by the Wizard of the North. Or we meet him in Edinburgh and Stirling, bathing in languorous memories of Mary Queen of Scots and the other old, sweet romances that the battlements of the Castles and the corridors of Holyrood so beautifully suggest. And we find him in the largest numbers in the Highlands, properly delighting in scenery as splendid as the world can show and looking anxiously for every cave and corrie that has possible associations with Bonnie Prince Charlie and Alan Breck and heroes dead so long ago.

That is the traveller's privilege, but it is one that the native cannot easily share. Of his history he may be, and

HADDINGTON ABBEY

usually is, proud. He does not forget. The old, sad story of his race is never far from his mind, and there is a background of dreams unfulfilled to all his thinking. But he has, after all, to live in his own age, and he must consciously or unconsciously resent the view of Scotland as a pretty museum-piece, as another Switzerland. He knows that all Scotland once lived intensely in its own right, and it discomforts him that so much of his country is a raree show and the rest of it a factory unvisited and seldom mentioned in polite society.

For that reason, because of this fantastic lack of balance in the national existence, it is well, even imperative, to look first at the Highlands, where the paradox of Scottish life is focussed like a scene upon a stage. If we look at the scenery only, and at the people as actors playing graciously against a decorative backcloth on the best Harker lines, we shall not even begin to understand Scotland. For a good deal of the heart of it is in these Highland people who, so agreeable, even so decorative, do not live where they do just that the visitor may be catered for and amused. They cannot all live as hotel-keepers, picturesque fishermen, gillies and postmasters. They are not there to run a holiday camp. It may be that they are doomed to do so, but it is not all they are fit to do, and it is assuredly not all they want to do. They do not all pine to go to the Lowlands, there to decorate the world as policemen and cook-generals. But it is very difficult for them to find good reasons for staying where they were born.

What a charming people they seem to the tourist! Their English is free from dialect and delivered with an exquisite intonation. They have a courtesy, a grace of manner, a hesitant delicacy hard to find in any other part of the British Isles. They seem always to defer, and haggling and disagreement even in the simplest matters of opinion appear to be beyond them. Isn't half the charm of a Highland holiday in one's small dealings with the people? What would a Highland holiday be, one wonders, if it were not for the personal contacts of the daily expedition to the Stores for the groceries and to the Post Office for the papers and the letters?

We all make a fine old song about escaping from the cares of everyday life, and we pretend solemnly that the need to order food is a bore and that newspapers are gross intruders on the solitude, but the fact is that we secretly cherish the necessity to break the monotony of *dolce far niente* and count the midday outing to the village one of the brightest moments of the diurnal round. It may be that in our heart of hearts we townsfolk are only bogus followers of the simple life, that we need that daily brush with the busy world to keep us sane. Certain it is that we get a purely sophisticated pleasure out of the simplicities and comedies of rural shopping in Highland places.

Let us imagine ourselves for a moment in a hamlet of Western Inverness, much patronised by knowing people from the South. This is none of your one-horse places where the Post Office is also the General Stores, and all is confusion when the morning mail comes in. No; we have the two establishments quite separate; and if the Post Office is a thought small and old-fashioned, you should just see Mr. Macphater's General Stores. A go-ahead man, Mr. Macphater had them done up in the spring. Up from Glasgow came a gang of shopfitters, and were given a free hand, so that you might now mistake the place for a corner of some multiple store, what with the granolithic floor, the cash-register and the patent ham-slicer.

Unhappily, you cannot alter the temperament of a race so easily as you can a fascia. It is all very well in the Post Office. That it should be jammed at noon is to be taken for granted, what with the crofter's boy from Lettermore getting the *Morning Post* intended for Miss Valentine at the Big House, and the latter's chauffeur protesting that his mistress does not take in *Meg's Paper*; what with Daft Jimmie Macdonald wanting a twopenny

15 WINTER IN GLEN CRERAN, BENDERLOCH, ARGYLL

16 THE WESTERN SEABOARD: the Panorama at Kentra Bay, Argyll

17 SPEYSIDE AND THE CAIRNGORMS: a Sombre Panorama over Miles of Highland Country

18 A WILD AND EMPTY COUNTRY: the Panorama of Ben Laoghal, Sutherland

19 A CROFTING TOWNSHIP AT STAFFIN, ISLE OF SKYE

20 MOUNTAIN AND FLOOD: the Sligachan River and Sgurr-nan-Gillean, Skye

21 OLD COTTAGES, CLACHAN OF BUNDALLOCH, WESTER ROSS

22 A LOVELY CORNER OF LOCH MORAR, INVERNESS-SHIRE

box of crayons while the Shooting Tenant's secretary has a parcel to register; what with campers clamouring for their letters, flappers squealing to know if their snaps have been printed yet, a small boy piping thinly but persistently for a penny comic and the two postmen-sorters arguing in Gaelic over an address written in violet ink by a Frenchman.

That is inevitable at the Post Office, even desirable from the holidaymaker's point of view, such a rare half-hour of excitement is it. But you would expect it to be all quite different behind Mr. Macphater's imposing façade, and that is where you make the mistake. Mr. Macphater is a go-ahead man, but he and his assistants are yet Gaels, and they are more than mere grocers. They may have a fancy red ham-slicer, but they still keep their Pan Drops in a drawer. While you are attempting to decide as between Cheddar and Dunlop with Mr. Macphater himself, one of his myrmidons excuses himself politely so that he may display to Mrs. Macinroy (from Rhu) a remarkable article of underwear in striped flannel. A lad buying artificial sand-eels, for the mackerel, is being elbowed out of his advantageous position at the counter by a woman from some remote croft bent on choosing a new waxcloth, while a large circle of assorted infants, each carrying a crumpled list of orders still to be filled, gathers round, open-eyed, to see the keeper from Back of Morrach fitted with a pair of light shoes for the Whist Drive and Dance in the Public Hall to-night.

Three assistants has Mr. Macphater, and he could do with fifteen at the rush hours and about twenty times as much counter-space, not to mention a brace of auxiliary ham-slicers. For, to be blunt, the Highland halflin is not very good at the grocery. Perfect in courtesy and genuine in anxiety to please, he is lamentably weak in method. Your bright lad in a city store would grab your shopping-list, make it up by himself, present you with a neat parcel in a trice and point to the cash desks.

It is not so in Macphater's. In these palatial premises

we proceed by numbers. "A pound of butter," you start off, meaning to make a business-like job of it, and before you can look up, Dougie has dashed off and is fighting with the proprietor for a place at the scales. You wait—two minutes perhaps—and Dougie comes back, panting but grinning, to handle the next item. So it goes on. One order puzzles him; he scratches his head with the butt of his pencil. "I'm not sure but we're out of tomatoes," he says sorrowfully; then, blithely: "Wait you! There'll mebbe be some in the store."

That means an absence of at least five minutes. And there are never any tomatoes in the store. You knew that, and Dougie knew that you knew, but the ritual must be carried out.

"Not a tomato in the place," announces Dougie cheerfully, returning, "but they'll be in with the goods on Wednesday about four."

Thus assured, you ask at last for the bill.

"What's the hurry?" asks the lad. "It'll do fine to-morrow. You're not going to run away from us."

It'll do fine to-morrow—always to-morrow. There is no hurry. Everybody trusts everybody else. It is all very amusing.

Quite so—but some of us must be forgiven if we discern a certain tragedy behind these easy-osy ways of Gaeldom. Mr. Macphater's display is very imposing, but if you look at it carefully you will find that it consists almost entirely of things in cans, cans that have come long distances to this delectable spot—mainly across the Atlantic. The cakes, the scones, the daily bread—they come from Glasgow. The fruit the holidaymaker wants comes from Glasgow; and the vegetables come—from the Gardens of England, or in cans. As for fish, you may whistle down the wind for days on end and never see a fin.

That is surely tragic. For this is not an infertile country. One does not need to be an agricultural labourer to know that the sandy soil could grow all the vegetables all the

23 A SLUM IN ARCADY

24 GROUSE MOORS NEAR ABOYNE, ABERDEENSHIRE

visitors of a good season could possibly consume. The coastal waters abound in mackerel and flounders and lythe, but no native will bestir himself to catch a few each day and turn a penny or two out of what would be a ready sale among housewives weary of offering their menfolk tinned tongue at every meal. Not one, although they live on the edge of poverty, will go out to fish for his own meagre table. The litter of cans along high-water mark tells the story.

Those romantic Highlands! Such sweet people, too marvellously amusing! Then we go back to the cities and rave about it all. Should we not think now and again of what we have imposed on the Highlands, with our cans and our summer lets that pay the rent and remove so much of the necessity for honest toil on the land and the seas?

It is quite wrong, however, to put it all down to laziness and leave it at that. The Highlander has shown himself in other fields to be a man of brilliance and energy. There is a helpful story, even if it be *ben trovato*, of an encounter between an elderly fisherman of Stornoway and the first Lord Leverhulme, who genuinely sought to understand why his schemes were unpopular with the natives. He enlarged on the prosperous future of Lewis and Harris as planned by himself, and begged the old man to imagine what splendid opportunities would lie before his own sons. "Yes," the ancient is said to have replied, "it's true that Donald and Seumas have a poor time of it, helping me at the fishing. But there's Peter now—he's a professor at McGill University in Montreal yonder, which they tell me is a great place for the learning. Then there's Iain—he's a doctor in Harley Street in London, which is well spoken of, and doing very well. And there's Angus—he's a magistrate in Burma, away beyond India. And Niall, the youngest. . ."

The legend expresses at once the truth and the tragedy of the Highlander. His talent has to be exported; in his own land he seeks in vain the means of self-expression.

It is a poor land, if beautiful, goodness knows, and the very means of living are hard to come by in it, but it once did support a proud peasantry that has degenerated to a sort of delicate defeatism. The clue to it all is in history—the smashing of the system natural to the people, followed by generations of landlordism in its most virulent forms. Even the hastiest traveller must encounter that blight in one form or another. Here he will be warned off a hillside and denied access to an alluring mountain, lest the grouse and deer be disturbed, there he will encounter a hamlet that has become virtually a cloister of gillies and estate servants, even its inn closed so that the itinerant stranger may not linger, and that there may be a place handy for an overflow of guests from the Big House.

Indignation comes easily to anybody who cares to contemplate the Highland scene as it is to-day, but it is best to curb it. Nobody has sinned with any great deliberation of evil, and the existing system is dying of its own inherent rottenness. All we observe at this juncture is that the Highlander remains subtly uneasy in the economy of modern Scotland. He has done magnificently abroad; he is the backbone of many a Lowland manufacturing town; but still in his own places he resists the ways of the new world. He may listen-in to Daventry National, but he will not have a Port Sunlight in the Outer Isles, and he calls for a "Day of Humiliation and Prayer" when the Traffic Commissioners grant to 'bus companies licences to run Sunday excursions through his land. Perhaps we can only explain the apparent paradox by saying that his defeatism is a sort of sullen pride, and that he has still an aristocratic tradition which will not allow Stornoway to become another Fleetwood. Who knows but that Lord Leverhulme was ultimately defeated because he arrogated to himself the sacred title of "Lord of the Isles"?

Yet the legend of the gloomy Gael is terribly misleading. His cast of thought may be wistful, taking colour

INVERNESS

from the sombre hills and the unresting sea (and certain popularised versions of his art have encouraged the misunderstanding), but he is in his natural state a being as cheery as any. His domestic tradition is one of the warmest hospitality, so that the institution of the *ceilidh* still flourishes—that gathering of neighbours round the fire, when song and jest and tale while away the long nights of the northern winter. It was a happy enough race that gave us those reels and strathspeys that are the merriest, liveliest and most urgent of dance measures. You need to spend a winter among them to understand the Highlanders and to know how they will forgather on the slightest provocation in communal festivity, and how a night of song and story will pass in the cheeriest way among them; so that they will not stop singing till the dawn.

There is in all Scots a dominant quality of desperation, of recklessness; the quality to which Mr. Walter Elliott once applied the excellent epithet "furious." It is common to both those groups we so loosely call Highlanders and Lowlanders. It may be the Celtic strain running through the race as a whole. But whether in his games or his song or his fighting or his roystering, nobody evinces it in more ebullient measure than those who sometimes seem to be living in twilight on the Celtic fringes.

The Highlands are momentarily in decay. The population dwindles alarmingly. Fewer and fewer speak the Gaelic tongue despite educational effort and the encouragement of An Comunn Gaidhealach, culminating each year in the fantastic excitement of the annual festival, the Mod. The economics of the day are all against the survival of the Highlander on his native heath; and if he disappears from that he will cease even to be an auxiliary in the imperial business. Against the total population of the country his numbers are few.

Yet he is the most significant of the Scottish phenomena. Gaeldom is remarkably homogeneous. The Barra fisherman may be a Catholic and the crofter of Ross a

25, 26 SPORTING RIGHTS: (*above*) a Typical Shooting Lodge near Tomintoul, Banffshire, and (*below*) Trophies of the Chase on the Duke of Portland's Stables at Berriedale, Caithness

27, 28 SPORT AND THE HIGHLANDER: (*left*) Bringing Home the Grouse from an Aberdeenshire Moor, and (*right*) a Strong Man at the Pitlochry Gathering

Wee Free Presbyterian of the most relentless order; the forester in Argyll and the gamekeeper in Sutherland may have some difficulty in understanding each other's Gaelic; and a Macdonald may to this day actually hate a Campbell. Yet they have held together wonderfully in their isolation, adhering to their own unique tradition and, in their own glens, defying the industrial advance, so that we too casually write them down as lazy and inefficient—seeing how they will mend a fence with the end of a derelict iron bedstead or sleep while the cut hay lies out under a threatening cloud.

They can do as well as any in the larger world of affairs, but they will not, or cannot, do much for themselves at home. They have given Scotland much, and yet resist the tradition of the Scottish majority. They represent, in short, a preposterous paradox, but one which is the key to the whole paradox of Scotland.

CHAPTER III

THE TRUE LOWLANDS

Highlands and Lowlands. . . . The phrase is almost exasperating in its capacity to mislead. In common usage, at all events, it has come to suggest that Scotland consists of the Highlands, at which we have just glanced, and a region given over hopelessly to industrialism. Whereas the Lowlands proper embrace vast tracts of rich and remote farming country, thousands of acres of high and stern land, lost hamlets and lone cottages, and a wealth of scenery as enchanting in its own way as that of the fabled region along the western seaboard. Once again there must be an insistence on the division of Scotland into three parts—Highlands, Lowlands, and the Industrial Belt.

It would be pleasant and profitable to speculate on the causes of popular indifference to the entity of these true Lowlands. It is as if they were taken for granted, though so many of the most notable and indigenous traditions of the people as a whole are rooted in them. The genius of a Scott could focus attention on a narrow strip along the line of the Tweed; though, by an irony, much of that strip is considerably industrialised. History lends magnetism to Stirling and Edinburgh, Falkland, and Kinross. Golf glorifies St. Andrews (even more than history and learning!) and the coasts of Ayrshire and the Lothians. Here and there a little place—a Peebles, a Moffat, a Dunbar, a Stonehaven, a Grantown-on-Spey, or a Nairn—makes its claim for distinction on the strength of natural attractiveness carefully developed. But so much else escapes the general notice. It is a fantastic paradox that the Solway coast and Galloway generally, regions of singular beauty and of infinite variety of beauty, get little or nothing of Glasgow's huge holiday crowds and are left to a handful of dis-

MOFFAT

cerning people from Tyneside. How comes it that Kirdcudbright, one of the sweetest towns in these islands, can remain the inviolate sanctuary of a colony of artists?

It is perhaps because such a province has, in a sense, been able for centuries to support itself and mind its own business. These are areas long tilled, equably managed, stable, and untouched either by the feverish exploitation of minerals or by the blight of sporting landlordism. They represent the solid norm of Scottish life, its background, foundations and all else that is permanent. This is the Scotland of Burns at his truest and best, the Scotland of the quiet, hard-working, gravely humorous men in hodden grey. It is one essential, and perhaps the more important, part of the dichotomy created by the existence within a small nation of two races and two languages.

And that even though the variations of blood, accent and outlook within it are far greater than within the compact community of the Highlands. As we shall see, the peasant of Ayrshire has much in common with the lad in the Aberdeenshire bothy; the soil gives them the same essential background; but their temperaments and habits of speech differ widely. There are quite dramatic variations of character among the constituents of the Lowland mass, and it is well that we understand these before we seek to define what it is they have in common that gives them their homogeneous strength.

Aberdeen is a legend of the universal type, and it is one solidly based on fact. If the tradition of meanness belies the people—and if the people themselves take a queer, contorted pleasure in inventing accretions to it—it rests on the truth about those strong and forthright folks who inhabit those three north-eastern counties of Scotland, Moray, Banff and Aberdeen, that make up the region compactly known as Buchan.

Here is a race eternally betrothed to the rich earth and racy of the soil. Predominantly Teuton as regards

29 WINTER ON A LOWLAND FARM

30 ANNANDALE, NEAR WAMPHRAY, DUMFRIES: a Pastoral Valley in the Southern Uplands

origin, the people have the sense of mundane values highly developed. The region, as it happens, has produced within recent years a proportionately large number of poets and novelists, but it could not be held that the Buchan farmer, his almost conventional adoration of Burns and small vernacular versifiers apart, worships any muses at all. He is forthright, literal, canny, pawky and hard—the Scot of a certain tradition to the *n*th power. He is coarse, and it is not without significance that the illegitimacy rate in that part of the world is abnormally high. Yet his coarseness implies the larger virtues of strength, simplicity and sincerity. And what he is as a man is oddly reflected in his speech, which is a hard, craggy, uncompromising affair of crashing consonants and high inflections. It may be studied in its purity in that small classic, *Johnny Gibb of Gushetneuk*, and there are a score of poets, Marion Angus, for instance, to demonstrate how curiously, on the other hand, it lends itself to an odd tenderness.

The temperaments and the accents soften as we go down the East Coast through Angus, the country of Barrie, and into Fife, where the honest brutality of Buchan gives place to a subtlety of caution, and the granite speech of Peterhead and thereabouts to a thinner, clipped delivery that would almost be a whine but for the rising, querulous inflections of it. "It takes a lang spoon to sup wi' a Fifer," says the metaphorical proverb, and it indicates the curious and unreasonable mistrust with which the natives of the Kingdom, as they are proud to call it, are regarded by their compatriots. Through the fat Lothians and down to Berwick, that fine town of uneasy destiny, the nip of easterly wind in temperament and speech prevails in varying degree. The Borders may be said to speak with the purely normal voice of Scotland, and there the people are strong, calm, courteous and grave. Towards Galloway a faintly Irish air comes over the scene, and the men and women of the huge dairy farms have large generosities superimposed on a definite narrowness in matters of faith. Turning northwards towards Ayr, we enter a region that is at once like and fantastically unlike Buchan, achieving, in short, the antipodes of this small but various Lowland world.

Burns has expressed Ayrshire for all time. The scene is easily envisaged: a pleasant if not highly distinguished pastoral country, studded with farms of a moderate size, though the small patches of industrialism that diversify it now had not developed in the time of the Bard. The scene, indeed, is not notably unlike that of Buchan, nor does the one people differ much from the other in those essentials that are common to peasantries the world over.

An Ayrshire ploughman, however, presents to the world quite another face than that sported by his brother from the austere North-East. In the matter of speech he is less precise, and the trend of his inflections is in the direction of a falling-away towards the ends of his sentences. That symbolises the standard contrast between East and West: everything clipped and hard and precise on the one hand, and untidy and soft and slovenly on the other. Probably it indicates the influence of the Gael in the West, and we shall see how the contrast is even more dramatically reproduced in the cases of Edinburgh and Glasgow. It may be remarked, by the way, that almost any novel of John Galt presents a faithful suggestion of the colloquial speech of Ayrshire before the influence of Glasgow got to work on it and an adequate presentation of the spirit of the people.

All this is not, of course, to say in effect that there is any ground for comparison in the matter of human generosity or of any other ultimate human value as between East and West, North and South, but it is at least worth noting that a solid peasantry includes such a considerable range of temperament. The variation of types encountered as we move round the coasts and borders of the country from Lossiemouth to Largs are, to be sure, infinitely more gradual and subtle than description can suggest. There are queer minglings and shadings

ABERDEEN CATHEDRAL

where the various influences have clashed. Thus the large and beautiful county of Perth is strangely lacking in character on the human side, its aboriginal quality squeezed out, as it were, by pressures from the cold East, the warm Highlands, and the industrial belt. The same is true, though in a lesser degree, of Stirlingshire. And while Renfrew and Dumbarton share something of the character of, say, Wigtown, they are largely industrialised and take much of their purely human nature from the adjacent Highlands. The confusion is most fantastically exemplified by the strange case of Lanarkshire which, in its Lower Ward, is the blackest corner of Scotland's Black Country, and houses a broth of races and, in its Upper Ward, rivals the remotest Highlands in the austere loneliness of its uplands—where one has encountered a shepherd who lives ten miles from the nearest habitation, sees hi kind once a week when he trudges over almost pathless moorland to fetch his provisions and, when asked to indicate the extent of his bailiwick, says simply: "The skyline."

One is indeed tempted in lighter moments to see a queer symbolism of Scotland in the dish that sometimes represents it in the eyes of lesser breeds without the law, the haggis. It is a small thing with a lot in it that is mysterious and not easily identifiable. But can we not also fairly say that it is a concoction with its own odd piquancy and curious interest? . . . Enough just now that those true Lowlands, so variously made up, hold together by virtue of the common possession of certain qualities. There runs through the whole complicated region a thread of what, baffled in the task of definition, one can only call inspissated Scottishness. And undoubtedly it depends for its strength and purity on being essentially a product of that common inheritance, the soil.

We are moving now among farming bodies, as they say, among those who, if not the flowers of Scotland's culture, are the salt of its earth. We have to think of mile upon mile of rolling countryside, dotted with the so

31 PETERHEAD, ABERDEENSHIRE: the Departure of the Fishing Fleet

32 A LOWLAND FARM IN SPRING

characteristic white walls of the slate-roofed steadings. It is the country of the poets—of the heavy-footed ploughman homeward bound, of rough dalliance among the corn-stooks, of Great Clydesdales straining at the plough with the seagulls wheeling over them, of quiet evenings in warm kitchens, of early beddings and early risings—with the radio nowadays mitigating the monotony and the ubiquitous 'bus bringing the meagre delights of the county a little nearer than they used to be.

In every one of these districts much of the farming is of the small, mixed sort, and in these two-pair-horse units resides the conservative backbone of the whole organism; but each region has its speciality and pride. Thus in Buchan they breed those dumpy favourites of the fat stock market, the black-polled Aberdeen-Angus cattle, and have a name also for horses of the Clydesdale breed. Through the Lothians, that rich, dry belt, the interest is in wheat, oats and potatoes; and hereabouts the farms are large, the dwelling-houses of them taking on the aspect of lesser mansions and their steadings notable in that every one boasts a somewhat surprising smokestack in brick.

The Galloway holdings run to size again, for this is rich pasture for the huge herds of cows that wander home in the evening, more than a hundred at a time, to yield the milk for a goodly proportion of the country's supply of cream and cheese. There is dairying in Ayrshire, too—the little town of Dunlop gives its name to an excellent cheese—and perhaps the most notable strain of Clydesdales originated here. But potatoes are once more grown in these parts on the grand scale, and it is a characteristic glimpse of the Scottish rural scene to see at work in the red fields the great, colourful bands of "howkers," mainly women and very often peripatetic Irish, who perform the hard tasks of digging and gathering.

It is to serve these rural parts that the finest of the Scottish towns exist, as it chances. The industrial region, naturally enough, has nothing like them—if, for con-

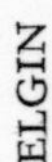
ELGIN

venience, we regard Edinburgh, Stirling and Aberdeen as being above the industrial battle. There are few towns in the Highlands, and they are mostly poor things, albeit on glorious sites. (The failure to make decent jobs of Oban and Inverness, so splendidly sited, would be in other circumstances a matter worth discussing.) As it is, such fine urban qualities as Scotland can boast are largely in these small, neat, clean communities that seem sometimes to be sleeping the centuries away, awakening only on market days and on Saturday evenings when the lads and lasses come in, even if it be only to "the pictures," from the farms and outlying hamlets.

Elgin is perhaps the best thing they have in the North-East, a curiously dignified place with a classical air about it, perhaps because its agreeable climate has always attracted the retired officer and imperial servant of the county class: just as Bath and Cheltenham and Tunbridge Wells contrive to give hospitality at once to eighteenth-century elegance and unreliable livers. Fife has St. Andrews, deriving, however, much of its real quality of enchantment from its political, ecclesiastical and academic associations. If Ayrshire has little to show in the way of fine towns, having been afflicted considerably by the diseases of industrialism—so that, indeed, it houses some of the vilest townlets in Scotland—there is in the Lothians Haddington, with its own haunting air of a small capital.

But it is the southern counties that boast the finest towns of all. Some of them have a name for distinction they do not quite deserve. Without the Abbey Melrose would appeal to the visitor in vain, and Jedburgh on a grey, wet day is no place to linger in. But there is Kelso, for all its share of industrialism a sweet town though hardly "the most beautiful if not the most romantic village in Scotland" the generous Sir Walter made it out to be. Such places as Annan, Lockerbie, Thornhill and Moffat witness in their different ways to the possession of grace in a byegone generation, some of them suggesting models for the modern town-planner. And there is always Kirkcudbright, singularly attractive at the mouth of the southern Dee, an ancient castle in the heart of it and a glimpse of beauty at almost every corner.

If a colony of artists have helped to keep Kirkcudbright lovely by jealously striving for the preservation of its native features, one wonders how it came originally to be a place of handsome houses with the quality of a Hampstead or a Boston, as if the Adam brothers had been given a free hand at the making of it. One can only predicate an enlightened laird of byegone days. The nineteenth century could never have created it. It is long since any laird in Scotland worked to establish beauty except in a toy bunch of model dwellings at his own castle gates.

In such towns, then, so many of them quite unknown to the traveller and generally ignored as a result of the absurd centralisation of the Scottish population in the industrial belt, there ebbs and flows a very normal, quiet, decent sort of Scottish life. It is a life of which the farming folk set the tempo, for many of them are markets merely, the minister, the doctor, the hotel-keeper and the larger shopkeepers forming the local eldership. You will come on one of them on an off-day, and it seems as if an enchantment of sleep had descended on some city half as old as time—and in the South Country they are apt to be rose-red, too, for the Old Red Sandstone of Dumfriesshire has gone to the building of many of them. The cars of voyagers rustle along their main streets, but a sleeping dog hardly stirs from his couch of warm dust in the middle of a roadway. Some small local picture-house will have its blueish lights sputtering in a darkened corner of an evening, but the tide of its patrons flows weakly on most nights, and all is quiet by half-past ten, save perhaps for a group of "characters" and youngsters talking in singularly loud voices at the corner by the Cross.

One wonders how the winter passes in such places, and yet it does so more pleasantly than the city-dweller

33 THE TWEED NEAR NEIDPATH CASTLE, PEEBLES

34 DUNKELD, PERTHSHIRE: the Typical Midland Village-Town

35 EYEMOUTH, BERWICKSHIRE: a little Fishing Port on the East Coast

36, 37 SWEET COUNTRY TOWNS: (*above*) Haddington; (*below*) Newton Stewart, on the Cree

might imagine. "The pictures" apart, there are the dances of this and that society, the bazaars and even those echoes of Victorian gaiety, the conversaziones. Perhaps the minister has visited the Holy Land during a vacation, and his lecture, with lantern-slides, is an agreeable standby. The touring lecturer, indeed, can command wonderful audiences in such places, and a musician of repute will attract a proportionately larger and rather more truly intelligent audience than he may in greater places. The local inns enjoy their orderly, garrulous trade. In summer the local golf-course (there is always one) carries its quota of mighty swipers before the Lord. Nowadays lawn tennis has gripped the younger folk everywhere. The wireless is at the command of the poorest, and strangely accented voices talk from great distances down every quaint alley. And there abides the tradition of domestic hospitality, so that there is a great coming and going among a people much more content with their lot than those of any Middle-Western Main Street.

Then on market days and Saturdays life leaps with a sudden urgency on the little towns, and happy activity stirs in the streets and shops. In come the County and the larger farmers in their cars, which lie parked in rich tiers in every street. There come old-fashioned bodies in gigs; and the Scottish rural scene is not fully comprehended unless in terms of the bicycles that bring all sorts and conditions to the weekly festival. The nowadays ubiquitous 'bus brings the rest, and the pavements creep with the hard-voiced ladies of the County in tweeds and sockettes, with farmers' wives in douce black, with the girls who have not studied the dress and deportment of Janet Gaynor and Mae West in vain, with large, hairy men in tight trousers and leggings, and with all the others who make up the typical rustic gathering.

The talk is loud and craggy and clear, as of people used to making themselves understood across the length of a field. The dealings are in the simplicities of food

KIRKCUDBRIGHT

and crops and bestial. It is the country in the town; and through those honest eyes you suddenly discover how many of the shops are given over to the provision of rural needs: to harness and shepherd's crooks and chicken-food and oilskins and incubators and gum-boots and the like. Those booths that cater for frivolity seem to wear a slightly amateurish air.

It is often argued that the modern influences, particularly of the cinema and the wireless, tend to upset the balance of this relatively simple life, but it could safely be held that the effect is quite in the other direction. The contact with the great world of cities has removed its mystery, and Jenny in Annan is as good as Jess in Glasgow. The statistics show a steady depopulation of the rural areas in recent years, but it has quite probably reached its highest point—if only because the plight of the thickly populated areas is a byword everywhere. If the mining town of Hamilton, say, is fated to decline, a Lockerbie or a Forfar may well increase as the dispossessed artisan tends to return to the soil. It is not without significance that a dramatic increase in the number of fruit- and vegetable-growers in the upper valley of the Clyde and a multiplication of the country's production of that type of commodity, with canning-factories springing up here, there and everywhere, is directly due to the unemployed collier's search for a new sort of living.

The illustration is perhaps topical, but it suggests a permanent effect—in fact, a general return to the conditions in which Scotland's pulse is most normal. And of all the factors making for this rediscovery of stability the 'bus is perhaps the most powerful. It at once increases and limits the individual's range, for when the means of travel are always there, the urge to adventure is always the less distracting. For the lad and lass in the farm of Cauldshields on the edge of the moor Glasgow ceases to be the dream of a lifetime and becomes the possibility of to-morrow, and so much the less exciting. The new influences may have stressed the littleness of Scotland, but they have also encouraged contentment among normal folk in the quieter regions of it.

And we cannot leave these small towns without noting that they do not by any means leave all the more spectacular glories to the Highlands. The Border towns particularly, perhaps just because of their proximity to the ancient enemy of England, have remembered that pageantry is in their inheritance, so that there has been a wonderful revival of native ceremonial: in itself a reaffirmation of the fundamental Scottishness. Galashiels, Hawick, Selkirk and other places are gay now at given seasons of the year with the crowds and bunting of a Braw Lads' gathering or the happy horsemanship and stirrup-cups of a Common Riding. Communal games still thrive, such as the handball of at least one Border town, played by scores of eager "Uppies" and "Doonies." Where local custom has fallen into disuse, they will go to their books and stage a pageant.

It is a healthy, a noble symptom. It tells of a Scotland in search of her youth and of comfort for her stricken heart. It is the first wave of a return to the Scottish normality, of which so much resides in these true Lowlands of the good farms and the small quiet towns.

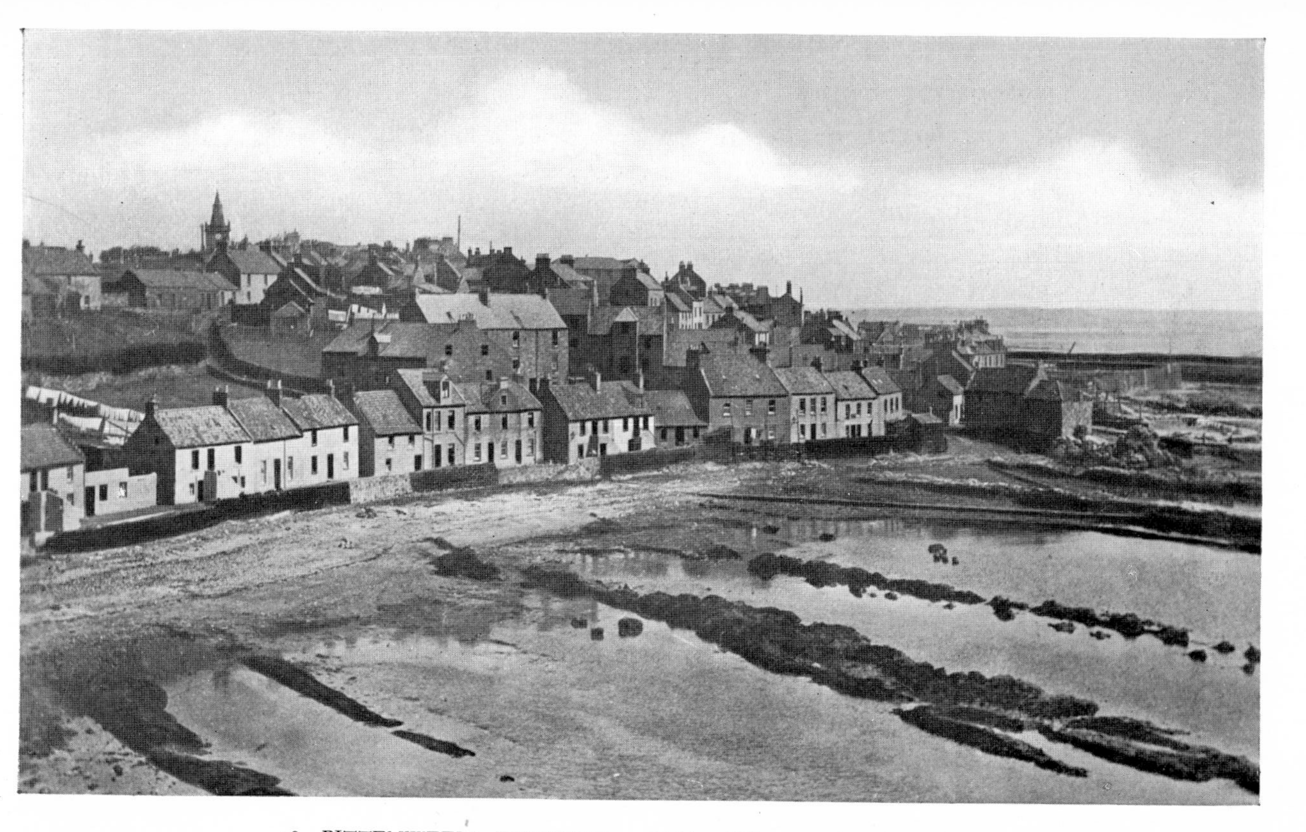

38 PITTENWEEM, FIFESHIRE: a Fishing Village on the Firth of Forth

39 ORCHARDS IN THE UPPER CLYDE VALLEY

40 THE PEACEFUL VALLEY OF THE UPPER CLYDE AT KIRKFIELDBANK

41 GLASGOW : the Docks

CHAPTER IV

BLACK COUNTRY

It used to be a strange experience, in the days of high prosperity, to come into Glasgow in the dark by the West Coast route from London. Carlisle left behind, the watcher at the carriage window of the train resigned himself to hours of travel through country utterly featureless in the night. Now and again the light in the kitchen window of some remote farmhouse would gleam for a space through the blackness or the oil-lamps of a country station stream past as the express bore northwards. There seemed to be desolation complete about the summit of Beattock, and for a time thereafter the unaccustomed voyager strove to resign himself to a chill passage through boreal emptiness. All the warmth and comfort of the gregarious South seemed very far behind.

Then, quite suddenly, great clusters of lights began to appear to left and to right, and the traveller stirred in his corner seat. Then his eye would be caught by the revolving wheels at some pit-head, lit by unsteady and lurid flame. He would sit bolt upright to see a row of purple flames, rising in weird beauty from conical, squat chimneys. Another row of flames, white this time and flaring in a curious static way from high smokestacks, might attract his gaze from the other side. And every now and again the train would rush, as it seemed, through a gigantic shed lit with fire so bright that the carriage-lights shone pallid and dull thereafter. Great and mysterious masses, like miniature alps, loomed against the night sky, their peaks fantastic.

It was like plunging into an inferno, a mad place of flame and fire-shot smoke and dark rites around pagan balefires, and the experience had the power to awe, until the reflective mind recalled the iron and coal and steel of

Scotland's Black Country, and the resigned passenger for Glasgow reached up to the rack for his kit.

Seen in daylight, this region was, and is, much as if fire and rapine had passed over it. It is a grey and littered countryside that heavy industry has blasted, and all the more depressing now that the tides of prosperity have receded from it, leaving a litter of abandoned works, grass-grown bings and yards, rusty iron and battered notice-boards behind. The streams are stained, the grass is dull, and the little towns one passes through have meanness written over them.

Yet this industrial region is certainly no uglier than any other of its kind in Great Britain. To the Scots eye, at least, it has a positive charm compared with that stretch of blackened plain between Warrington and Preston, where the monotony of red brick seems to accentuate the gloom. For there is always a hill hereabouts, lifting a cheerful crest to the sky with, probably, a tuft of trees upon it; and agriculture has never been evicted from that valley of the Clyde. In the very heart of Bellshill, an unhappy town that symbolises in Scotland the extremes of industrial degradation, there is still a farm, and the ploughs labour in the shadows of the slag-heaps everywhere. The mining village of Larkhall is ringed round with pits, and yet a country of wooded enchantment lies just behind it above the Avon. Out of a mean street of mean houses and multiple shops you can almost step into the policies of Bothwell Castle, a demesne as gracious as Scotland has to show. Hamilton can still boast its ducal park, though the cracked relics of the Palace are, by a bitter irony, rapidly subsiding into the earth from which a goodly proportion of the ducal wealth has been hewn.

These sudden paradoxes of scene and feature indicate at once the swiftness of industry's development during the early decades of the nineteenth century and the incompleteness of industry's victory over Scotland, albeit it has imprisoned about half the population within a mere strip

42 SHIPBUILDING AND SUGAR: the Vista of Greenock on the Firth of Clyde

43, 44 HUMBLE LIFE: (*above*) a Croft in Ardgour, Argyll, and (*below*) a Miners' Row in Lanarkshire

of country. Those hills rising above the blackened landscape seem to testify to the persistence of something aboriginal and enduring, just as the people of the small, black towns—though they have been subject for generations to the same influences as industrial populations everywhere and though they are racially bastards, with a strong element of Irish in their blood—are yet inveterately Scottish. The temptation is to set the industrial Lowlands apart as a special compartment of the country colourlessly peopled; and they certainly constitute a special problem; but at least it can be said with certainty that in these teeming valleys the whole, daft range of the Scottish qualities, from whichever of the particular racial sources, is to be found in its ultimate completeness. The Coatbridge man, let us say, stands with the crofter of Skye and the shepherd of Peebles as a representative Scot in his own right. We may deplore, but we cannot explain away, our melting-pot.

Startlingly swift was the development of this region and brief, as history is measured, its heyday. Defoe lived not so very long ago, and he described Glasgow as "the beautifullest little City I have seen in Britain." That was in 1723, or thereabouts, when the town had a population of about 15,000. Now Glasgow has a population of over a million, and that it is the beautifullest city to be seen in Britain is the last claim one could possibly maintain on its behalf. The population of Paisley multiplied itself ten times in seventy years or so; the inhabitants of Coatbridge achieved the same feat within the twenty years between the 'thirties and 'fifties of last century as the uses of coal and iron and steam-vessels became familiar—and profitable—to man. One could, indeed, go on quoting figures that, examined with a thought to what they mean in terms of humanity, are as dramatic as economic history has ever produced. It was in Scotland a convulsion, this industrial revolution, and it affected every corner of a small country. It had peculiarly strange and extravagant results.

What it must have meant in the way of racial confusion should be clear by now. (It is an old legend that there are more "Campbell's" than "Smith's" in the Glasgow Directory. True or not in fact, it expresses a racial truth.) What it meant in the way of rapid expansion of towns should be obvious. If we can envisage all the implications of this sudden development—the clash and fusion of unsympathetic racial strains, the absence of any tradition to control the lay-out of the new towns and the architectural adventures of the exploiters of the situation—we shall cease to sniff as we pass through, say, Holytown, and darkly wonder that mankind should be such a willing partner in its own spiritual disintegration.

There is no getting away from it that greed—or, shall we say, "the economic urge"?—made these industrial Lowlands what they are. While the money was good, nothing else mattered much. Beauty notably cowered in the furthest corner of the national consciousness. The aristocracy had lost interest in the immediate fate of the country and, having an expensive row to hoe at the Court of St. James's, was delighted to discover a ready source of income in mining royalties and in the feuing of land for new building. Yet the economic sins of the landlords were perhaps as nothing to their sin of omission represented by the removal through their absence of traditional order. Such order as prevailed in the villages that were to become grey and smoky towns was not strong enough to meet the new and gigantic forces so largely released by a Scotsman, James Watt. Thanks to the accident of history, there was little enough of tradition left in the Scotland that was overtaken by the industrial revolution; the new Scotland developed quite independently of tradition.

The results of this preposterous confusion are most easily understood in terms of the towns the men of the new age created—or, rather, suffered to arise. It is difficult and dangerous to generalise about a people, even about a relatively small group of people, but the group of build-

45, 46 GREY DAYS IN GLASGOW: (*above*) a Typical Tenement Court, and (*below*) Street Scene in the Gallowgate

47 THE RETURN TO WORK: a Happy Crowd at Clydebank, with the Giant "534" in the Background

48 "No. 534" IN THE MAKING: at Work on the Giant Cunard-White Star Liner at Clydebank

49 A SATURDAY ON THE SANDS AT PORTOBELLO, NEAR EDINBURGH

ings which they have set up, and in which they are content to live, forms an exact enough measure of their spiritual state. And at once we can say that industrial Scotland is not, in the delicious American phrase, easy to look at. The background may be more agreeable than that of the Lancashire plain or than that of the blasted area that has Birmingham as its nexus, but comparisons in degradation are unprofitable, and there are about so many of the Scots towns a meanness and greyness that England at its worst does not seem able to rival. This effect of sordidness is due in part to climate, which at once dictates that the houses shall be built of stone instead of brick, and that they shall be of heavy structure. It is due in part to the system of land ownership. For the rest, the aesthetic crime must be set down to the charge of a people robbed by circumstance of tradition.

The dearness of the land produced some of the worst effects of degradation in the long run. It should be explained that the Scots system of land tenure differs considerably from that of England, the "feu" being the product of a simple contract between landlord and tenant whereby a lease in perpetuity is established. It has the vast advantage over the English leasehold system of avoiding the ruinous "falling in," but it had certainly the disadvantage in the bad days of allowing the landlord to insert somewhat exigent conditions in the contract, and, in the days of wholesale and haphazard building, to charge sweetly for the use of a plot of ground. One knows of villas in certain West Coast towns that, sizable as they may be, have to bear ground burdens so extremely onerous that their occupation in modern times is beyond all save the very rich—who do not choose nowadays to live in suburban villas—and so that they either lie empty or are being demolished, their quite moderate gardens cut up into smaller building plots. It is only within the last twenty years or so that there was abolished by statute the iniquitous system whereby, at stated periods throughout the duration of the feu, every 19 years as a rule, the landlord exacted a "triplicand"—that is, three times the normal feu duty.

It was an age of exploitation all round. Of the system slums were an inevitable product. It happened over and over again, notably in Glasgow, that two or three tenement buildings would be set up in close-gathered rows on a feu originally intended for one, the property-owner carrying on the work of social ruination at a time when accommodation had to be provided for the hordes of incomers to the industrial field and nobody had the time or knowledge or enlightenment to give thought to the future. The result, of course, was overcrowding, with all its resultant effects on health and morals. Thus the slums of Glasgow, for instance, became notorious, too many of the people stunted in bodily and mental growth, and a problem established that is not yet solved. So also about the pits something very like slavery put the colliers and their families into those long, bleak, squat insanitary rows that were virtually barracks and still house too large a proportion of the population. The dearness of land finally produced that most characteristic feature of the Scottish urban landscape, the tenement.

That the tenement is an undesirable form of communal dwelling it would be quite absurd to maintain. In the inner suburbs of Glasgow, for instance, it is easily seen that it can be a clean, attractive, convenient and not ungracious item in a city's housing equipment. Manifestly it can be a horror where the constituent apartments are small, the number of the tenants to the block high, and the landlord a mere collector of rents. Otherwise its influences are spiritual. Plainly built of dark, grey stone, long rows of tenements make many Scottish streets seem like canyons in a deserted land of gloom. They oppress the spirit. The domestic life that glows so warmly within would seem to acquire its qualities of cosiness and kindliness from sheer reaction to the unfriendliness of the cliff-like exteriors.

The dullness of the average small town in industrial

50 A MILL TOWN IN TEVIOTDALE: Hawick from the Air

51 CROFT-HOUSES, OLD AND NEW, AT GEIRINISH, SOUTH UIST

52 THE FISHING TOWNLET OF INVERALLOCHY, ABERDEENSHIRE

Scotland suggests one of fate's most cynical conspiracies. It is hard to find one of the lesser places depending on coal and iron that differs much from another. In Lanark and Fife they seem to be all length and no breadth—small houses and tenements strung along an endless Main Street, with an outcrop of Old Red Sandstone on an ambitious shop frontage breaking the monotony here and there and a certain liveliness about the inevitable Cross. There will be a few small villas to house the officials and foremen of local enterprises and the more prosperous shopkeepers, notably the manager of the Co-operative Society. One large villa houses the doctor, another is at once the office and dwelling-house of the banker. Churches in various versions of bogus Gothic testify to the denominational zeal of the Scot, and in most mining districts the Chapel, as the Presbyterian describes the Roman Catholic Church, is liable to be a prominent landmark. (Writings on the walls, referring unpleasantly to the Pope, testify to the abiding strength of religious passions in the descendants of the Covenanters.) There will be a football field somewhere behind the tedious rows of dwellings and probably a bald quoiting pitch. Throw in a public park with some iron swings for the children and a picture-house with a façade in battered stucco, and the picture is more or less complete.

Such towns are creations of the industrial age, and a good deal more sorrow than anger must be brought to the contemplation of them. It is vastly more distressing to consider how in Scotland many ancient towns, once full of historical interest and buildings in the pure native style, have been overwhelmed by the fungoid growth of Victorian ugliness. Perhaps Dumbarton is the most tragic case in point—a town that should have ranked with Edinburgh and Stirling for distinction, if only because like these it stands in the shadow of a dominant Rock, the westernmost of the curious chain of three that stretch across the narrow waist of the country and were such powerful factors in its history. A town-planner might dream for years of the ideal site and never come on a better. The pleasant delta of the Leven—the "pure stream" to whose "translucent wave" Tobias Smollett paid patriotic tribute—is beautifully encircled by high romantic hills. The town is at the bridgehead of that fine river where it makes an alluring S-bend just before it joins the Clyde in the shadow of the Rock. Here should have been a town in a thousand, and here actually is one of the meanest towns in Christendom; whether you see it, as a bird would, from the western peak of the Rock or from the main road to Loch Lomond and the West of which the High Street is a part.

The bird's-eye view reveals the chief factor in the making of the modern town what it is. This is a great and historic shipyard that occupies such a remarkably long stretch of the river frontage that the burgh has been pushed back, as it were, from its natural site, with the converse result that the Rock, as seen from the town, dwindles in significance and has little or no relationship to the place to which it gives its name. Just so, one can hardly doubt, was it the rapid development of the shipyard during the nineteenth century that produced the architectural chaos that is the High Street of Dumbarton to-day. That street runs in what should have been an enchanting curve round the back of the sheds and the fitting-shops to join the Leven some hundreds of yards from its mouth; and, shipyard or no shipyard, it might still have been fine had the merest shadow of a plan gone to its making. Now it is just a tragic mélange of mingled and competing styles, all the more hideous since it stands in contrast to the austerity of the old Kirk that, itself a miracle of the style known bitterly as Heritor's Gothic, almost takes on an antique dignity in comparison with the Victorian frontages.

It so happens that the ghastliness of this High Street is emphasised by the survival in the middle of it of one genuinely antique building. This, typically, is occupied as the showrooms of the local gas undertaking, but it

53 DUMBARTON: the Sad Surroundings of the Castle Rock

54 HIGHLAND GAMES

55 DOLE QUEUE

56 AN EAST END PLAYGROUND IN GLASGOW

57 PUBLIC-HOUSE INTERIOR

58 INDUSTRIAL FIFESHIRE: Bowhill Collieries and Village

stands out with the gracious dignity of a lady among trollops. It wears a Flemish air, and its crow-stepped gables suggest a tradition, and one can dream of a sweep of such buildings replacing the shabby fretwork of the street as it is. But one dreams in vain. Too much of what was good in Scotland went under the hands of exploiters in a hurry, and it is to be feared that there is not in the heart of Scotland to-day very much sense of what was fine in the past. That battle is lost, and we can write the defeat down as the vilest consequence of the discovery of the coal that is being worked out and of the iron that is almost utterly exhausted. And there is nothing left.

The sense of the overweening weight of that spiritual and material débris must oppress the observer of the Scottish scene. It may seem unfair to concentrate on Dumbarton, but nowhere in Scotland is the industrial tragedy so conveniently symbolised. How, short of a conflagration, could its state be remedied by the most enlightened will? Who will tackle those abandoned works in foul red brick that must come down sooner or later? Who will demolish a bogus Gothic erection in a side-street—a building which, serving as a public hall, is an architectural fraud and has only a rabble of mean tenements for its setting? Who will remove the hideous German guns before the Old County Buildings in the same street and let the world see that they have at least some classical decency? Who will realise that the not utterly intolerable Municipal Buildings—Scots Baronial in Old Red Sandstone—need a better setting than that provided by a railway line and two or three sombre little terraces?

Whatever virtues we may find in the people who have to live in such an environment, we shall not find the sense of fitness. The concentration is on the hard values of the struggle for existence. It is a rough, slightly sombre, downright people that inhabits these blackened regions. Of social grace they have next to nothing; their scorn of the graces is indeed terrific. On the other hand, they have the virtues of domesticity highly developed. The fireside clime matters much to them and, behind a great shyness in intercourse that makes them seem inhospitable to the utter stranger, they are in reality kindly to a fault. They have the sense of all but aesthetic values; they are fierce in defence of their rights; but with that goes an abundant sense of the rights of others. It is not without significance that the industrial lowlands of Scotland are the traditional home of Radicalism. It is not without meaning that admiration of the poems of Robert Burns develops among them as bardolatry. It seems paradoxical, this juxtaposition of violent political feeling and warm sentiment, but it is surely a direct product of history. Those who cannot trace the connection might do worse than study the very typical career and curiously attractive personality of Mr. David Kirkwood.

But it would be wrong to dismiss the people of the dark towns as lacking in culture altogether. They have a culture all their own, and no negligible one it is. One remembers a day in Gallipoli, many years ago now, when word reached a Clydeside battalion, then in rest camp, that a barge had been shelled and holed at W Beach; and could they do anything about it if the authorities provided the material? Then it was a miracle to see how soldiers suddenly became artisans again, and rolled up their sleeves with a sort of grim joy, and demanded to be led forthwith to "the job." Down on the beach they reverted to type, delighting in the familiar task. A private with a bad military record would reassume his status as an expert riveter and take to ordering his corporal about. The dry orderliness of military discipline was replaced by the finer ritual of technical efficiency. It was the industrial Scot expressing himself to the full, "getting on with it," in his own urgent phrase. It is a mighty tradition, and lovely in its own way. It creates loveliness in great ships and smooth and complex machinery. Nowadays we may be unwilling to admit it, but "Macandrew's Hymn" was not a product of mere romanticism.

It is not that the typical Scot of the industrial belt can be pinned down and exhibited like a butterfly on a card. The social divisions have developed with the years. The region has its magnates of Big Business, gradually losing their racial quality through educational and commercial affiliations with England. It has its vast and finely graded middle classes, its dull substratum of Irish labour, and even its Glasgow gangsters. All these we shall encounter in due course. It is enough in the meantime, however, that the divisions are infinitely less clearly marked than they are in older and more feudal societies, and that that bastard aggregation of all the Scottish elements, with a few from outside thrown in, has acquired a character which, differing strangely from those of the pure Highland and pure Lowland strains, is nevertheless compact and the most dominant in the Scotland of to-day.

CHAPTER V

A TALE OF FOUR CITIES

The four great cities of Scotland are, in order of size, Glasgow, Edinburgh, Dundee and Aberdeen. Together they hold nearly half the population of Scotland. Glasgow alone shelters more people than the other three put together. While the last Census showed a steady, and in some cases alarming, decline in the populations of the rural counties, the same set of figures showed that the city populations still tend to increase.

A brief study of these facts should make it clear that, considering its size, Scotland is overweighted with cities. Outside London, no other city in the British Isles is so big as Glasgow; and Glasgow is larger in the Scottish scale than London is in the English, while, in the same proportion, Edinburgh, Dundee and Aberdeen are swollen giants as compared with, say, Birmingham, Leeds and Bristol within the English economy. The size of the cities is the most obvious symptom of the hopeless lack of balance in Scottish life. The influence of the cities is too great. We have reviewed most of the causes that produced this effect, and now we may well look to see how these absurd aggregations of people variously affect the country as a whole.

It can be said at once that there is not a Scottish city but differs spiritually from the three others in the most marked degree. You could hardly pass at random through a concourse of human beings and pick out four individuals more strongly assorted. We look for well-marked character in the Scot, and we know that he can present one or two, or even three, characters—Highland or Lowland or some curious blend of these in their infinite permutations and combinations—but if the student would quickly grasp the outlines of a complicated system, he would do worse than confine himself to an intensive

59 DUNDEE FROM ACROSS THE FIRTH OF TAY

60 DUNDEE, THE TAY BRIDGE, AND THE COAST OF FIFE

study of the Scot as he exhibits himself in his four most populous centres. If it be observed that there is no Highland town of size, the answer must be that Glasgow is that: a fact which strangely complicates and adds to the interest of that community.

If comparisons are permissible, it would be said by any detached observer that the four places of our regard are not equal in force, as distinct from variety, of character. Nobody could hesitate to say that Aberdeen, for instance, presents to the world the most compact and uncompromising aspect of all, and few would deny that Dundee seems to be much less definitely assertive than its rivals.

This is, indeed, a curious case. It is an East Coast town with a West Coast temperament. It is a big place without any distinguishing marks save its somewhat strange political history during recent years and certain other associations that do not, however, seem to have grown naturally out of its essence. It is something to have returned to Parliament within twenty years or so both Mr. Winston Churchill and a Prohibitionist so austere as Mr. Edwin Scrymgeour; and a reputation for the production of marmalade is not easily come by. But, remembering the Tay Bridge, its uniqueness and its history, we do not naturally remember that its northern terminus is Dundee; nor does the mere mention of the name immediately produce a mnemonic as that of Aberdeen suggests granite at once, or that of Edinburgh a hundred aspects of history, or that of Glasgow a legend of revolutionary politics. Some of us are apt to think of Dundee merely as the city whose fathers not long ago knocked down an ancient building of unique loveliness in almost pig-headed defiance of universal protests. Dundee has lost its Town House for ever, and what it has gained is known only to the Gods.

It is no mean city, for all that. It stretches agreeably along a hillside above the estuary of the Tay. It has a history. It gave its name to a gallant soldier and a gallant song. In the Town Churches it has a building of the most unusual character, a great cruciform pile that, dominated by the fine Old Steeple, houses three parish churches under one roof. And yet, once again, the modern Dundee does not exist at all on the strength of that past. One fancies that it would choose to be judged on the strength of what it is, a municipality up to date and "improved" —even to the extent of the demolition of its rarest building. In short, the city might be said to have renounced its Scottish birthright and to have become in consequence what diplomacy calls a *heimatlos* alien: neither quite one thing nor the other.

For this queer lack of character in Dundee certain factors can be held to account in part at least. For one thing, it looks to the east and has been seduced to some extent and through its whaling and shipping connections by the Scandinavian heresy. But the fact that its staple industry is the preparation of jute is assuredly at the bottom of it all. For this traffic in an exotic material has attracted its eye away from Scotland. If Edinburgh is apt to look to London for a lead, Dundee looks to Calcutta. Much of its money was made overseas. Many of its sons plan their whole careers in terms of Bengal. The communal drive tends furth of Scotland, and in the achievement of very considerable prosperity—which has given the town a lavish endowment of public buildings—a deal of native character has been lost. Add the fact that the mills have attracted the labouring Irish in large numbers, and the relative colourlessness of the community by the Tay is explained as nearly as such imponderables may be.

But perhaps we can agree that few communities could survive a comparison with the almost menacing vigour and directness of Aberdeen, so well and truly named the Granite City. Here is an attitude to life quite clear and uncompromising and self-reliant, not to say forceful. That may again be accounted for by reasons fairly obvious. The city serves a region of which the aboriginal racial strain has remained marvellously intact, securely

61 ABERDEEN: the Harbour and Skyline

62 THE GRANITE CITY: a Bird's-eye View of Union Street, Aberdeen

63 ABERDEEN: a Street in the Old Town

64 ABERDEEN: the Fish Market

65, 66 CLASSICAL VISTAS AT (*above*) EDINBURGH, (*below*) GLASGOW

based on a soil passing rich. There is neither coal nor iron within miles. Big as it is, Aberdeen is still a county town and otherwise dependent on a factor equally stable and traditional—the sea fisheries. It is remote up there in the north-eastern corner of the country and free from the influences that pull the communal minds of Edinburgh and Glasgow towards the South. That Aberdeen tends to look towards London rather than towards the industrial Lowlands is, in fact, the measure of her Scottish independence. She looks on London as an equal and not as an entity to be aped as, it may reasonably be feared, Edinburgh does.

One is tempted to wonder if the native granite, as well as providing the most convenient of symbols, has affected the spirit of the people and entered their souls. A psychologist might very well hold that the act of living among the silvery austerities produced by the communal use of that stone orders the minds of men along channels clearly marked. All we can say as outsiders, however, is that the granite makes for splendid effects. The newer parts of Aberdeen on a clear, wintry morning have a hard sparkle that gives the place a quality utterly different from any other town on earth, unless it be Helsingfors. It has distinction. It has quality. Here, you say to yourself, is a city that, whatever its faults, is something existing in its own right and on its own unaided strength. In certain moods it seems just too hard and clean for the comfort of normal human beings; in others it suggests stability and a sort of drab strength. Never are you in doubt as to its purposefulness.

Taking it by and large, Aberdeen does not notably give the stranger the impression of either warmth or ease. The ostensible mood is quite definitely cold. Perhaps ten minutes devoted to the study of the external aspects of Marischal College, the most prominent building in the town, is as educative from the stranger's point of view as the most systematic survey of the communal elements. There, it seems, is all Aberdeen in one lump of stone.

It is handsome. It is austere. It declares itself in unequivocal terms. It is classical. And yet it is somehow a thought too reserved. It will not go the whole hog, and it refuses to be frankly communicative. There is always, in everything Aberdonian, something slightly chilling; something even a little grudging; so that softer breeds without the law are perhaps to be forgiven if they find in contact with the native something unapproachable, even unfriendly, behind that notable façade of downrightness.

Nor is granite the only symbol this coldly splendid city offers to the outer world. No view of the place has any validity if it does not embrace the Fish Market. That astonishing sight has to be witnessed in the morning fairly early, when a mile of concrete, as it seems, is littered with the glacial harvest of the sea and men are buying and selling and handling, with an easy familiarity, the cold and dead things that are to feed the millions to-morrow. It seems a frozen jungle of fish—haddock, cod, hake, squids and whatnot, laid out carelessly for the allurement of the men with the money to buy. And by such a traffic, one thinks—by this hard dealing in forms that are really exquisite—the spirit of Aberdeen seems to be powerfully affected. Something of the coarse, cold salt, something of the ruthlessness of the North Sea, has entered the blood. Men must work, and women must weep. There is little time, one fancies, for the softnesses.

But when all that is said and done, Aberdeen is capable of the old Scots trick of surprise. There is, after all, a beating heart behind the shining armour. For out of the modern city you can pass within a few minutes to Old Aberdeen where everything is suddenly soft and red-tiled and old. Here are quaintly named and haplessly wandering streets of antique charm. Here is King's College, its weathered sandstone like a sweet nut within the carapace of granite. Through the old streets move singularly handsome lads and lasses in the short red gowns of the

67 "AULD REEKIE": the Spires and Chimneys of Edinburgh seen from Murrayfield; Arthur's Seat in the Background

68 EDINBURGH: the Westward View down Princes Street from Calton Hill

bajan, the undergraduate. The Chapel of King's College would notably ornament Oxford.

All this is not just an expression of the Scots' devotion to learning. It is a richer and finer thing than that. It is a survival of the true Scotland, nobly and inexhaustibly breasting the waves of what we call Progress. With the University of St. Andrews, King's College represents the real thing and that which we must now call the what-might-have-been. The point is that it survives behind the glitter of the granite; and on the strength of that alone we may safely say that Aberdeen is the most Scottish of the Scottish cities; even a good deal more so (if a neutral may hazard the opinion) than Edinburgh, the Capital, itself.

That Scotland has one of the loveliest capitals in Europe is the merest commonplace, taken for granted. That Princes Street is one of the loveliest streets in Europe is a generalisation on the lips of every traveller—though the distinction of that thoroughfare is really a little more questionable than the beauty of the town as a whole. If one can imagine Princes Street existing in space as a thing by itself, there would be nothing but derision for it as an aesthetic entity. It is really a lamentable row of buildings that faces the Castle Rock, even a disgrace. The beauty of the street rests on elements, in the creation of which fallible Man had no part whatsoever. It is made by the noble dominance of the Rock. It is a geological accident merely that it is an esplanade, open to the sun on one side. If the community had dealt faithfully with Nature there would still be a sheet of water between Princes Street and the Rock. But they drained the Nor' Loch so that a railway line might run through the city to terminate at one of the ugliest hotel buildings in Europe. All of which is worth remembering, lest we be tempted to give the community more credit than is strictly its due.

It is simply a fact that the best of Edinburgh comes out of history and tradition. The newer extensions of the city do not suggest that the municipality is any more jealous of its inheritance than others less happily endowed. It is sprawling like the rest, breaking out in a peripheral rash of building-schemes; and certain recent developments in the ancient heart of the town—notably the mean allocation of a site for the National Library—show that conservatism, so mindful of the past, has not always a generous eye to the future.

The spirit of Edinburgh seems in detachment just a little like that—a little complacent, a trifle haughty, considerably snobbish; regarding itself on the whole as being a cut above the Scotland of which it is the administrative centre. Were a genuine movement towards Scottish independence to sweep the country—as is always on the cards—Edinburgh would assuredly be the last place to hold out for the association with England. Itself richly endowed with historical schools, it secretly believes that Eton and Sandhurst are the repositories of all decency. And now its native schools take their tone from the South the community secretly envies and sedulously apes.

But need we wonder that such a lovely town should turn its back, as it were, on the country it governs? In Scotland it is *hors concours*, so very much finer than anything else within hundreds of miles of its boundaries. It represents what Scotland ought to have been throughout, and it is hardly to be blamed for looking at the rest and saying, however unconsciously: "What am I doing in this galley?" Though it may have its industries—a prosperous brewery abuts on the Palace of Holyroodhouse—it is essentially a survival. Traditional buildings fret the skyline down the length of the Royal Mile from the Castle to the Palace—"the braw hie-heapit toun" of Lewis Spence's exquisite fancy. Even where it calls itself New (for we can charitably ignore the Victorian horrors of Princes Street in the meantime) the essential Edinburgh has an exquisite elegance of the eighteenth-century sort, there being little in all Europe to vie with the austere dignities of George Street, of Hanover and

69, 70 OPPOSITE SHORES OF THE FIRTH OF FORTH: (*above*) a Corner of the Docks at Leith; (*below*) an Old Street at Culross, Fife

71, 72 MEDIEVAL EDINBURGH: (*left*) Fisher's Close, a typical "wynd"; (*right*) Old "Lands" near the Castle

Charlotte Squares and of the oval about Moray Place. That is all superb, deliciously urbane. The sight of the tumbling Firth of Forth from the ridge along which George Street runs seems a vulgar if delicious intrusion on a civilised decorum.

We may react against a certain chill smugness in the bearing of Edinburgh towards the meaner world—"East-windy, West-endy," the irrepressible John McNeill christened it—but here is a quality which, however out of key with the tone of modern Scotland as a whole, is absolutely invaluable to Scotland. It is the quality of permanence, of grace, of order. It comes of long and familiar dealing with the larger affairs of a nation. Here sit the Senators of the College of Justice—such a glorious term!—presiding over the Supreme Courts. Here flourishes the Bar, with special sorts of solicitors ministering unto its members. Here most of the banks and the more monumental insurance companies have their headquarters. (Could anything be more impressive than the Scottish Widows' Fund, under which title one famous provident company operates in a superbly dignified manner?) That is the note—tradition, security, safety first; and it is quite remarkable how the official coterie—with, one imagines, a nice taste in claret—has contrived to dominate Edinburgh even into these restless days of technology. In the Capital of Scotland the upper middle classes set the pace and rule the roost.

Now, it is a very strange thing indeed that what we must call, for mere convenience, the lower orders of Edinburgh are quite singularly lacking in distinctive character. It is as if they have no abiding place in such an elegant town and are rather conscious of the fact; or it may be that the working class is an infinitely smaller proportion of the population than it is apt to be elsewhere in Scotland. At all events, this apparent eclipse of the character of the common people in the Capital marks the essential difference between it and its neighbour and rival of the West, Glasgow.

Glasgow is big—really much too big for Scotland. It sprawls. It has grown almost anyhow, without plan and without regard for tradition. That Glasgow is absurdly maligned would be a thesis very easy to defend. It is not by any means all degradation. It has its own vistas of wild beauty, its own grim dignity, and many unsuspected sweetnesses. Its ill-luck is to fail in any comparison of its amenities with those of the lovely city only forty miles away. Neither geology nor history has assisted it in this matter of looks. What the geologists call its clay drumlins give its West End an odd character of variety and even charm, and sentiment can see it as a City upon Seven Hills, with the storied Clyde cutting a silver filagree through the smoky maze of it. But these are mere possibilities forsworn. What it might have been is hopelessly overbalanced by what it is—square mile upon square mile of meanness and untidiness, of greyness and unnecessary squalor, of elements strangely diversified and quite unrelated. It is a city so chaotic that one despairs of discovering a generalisation to come within measurable distance of describing its quality. If it has the faults inherent in a fairly recent industrial growth, it has the interest of diversity. He would be a poor observer who did not see in Glasgow one of the most diverting communities in Christendom. But neither the most devoted loyalty nor the most exacting passion for accuracy could reasonably quarrel with the average stranger's impression of it as a grey and formidable city in its outward aspects.

This impression is curiously fortified by the dress and deportment of the people. The proportion of artisans and labourers to the total population being so high, their tweed caps and drab clothes sound a peculiarly low note in a subdued colour scheme. The business man of this strange city has an incorruptible devotion to the bleak rigidity of the bowler hat. Even in the height of summer the girls on whom one would reasonably depend for a touch of gaiety must wear over their most alluring dresses an overcoat of some forbidding sort. Such is one of the

73 THE BUSINESS HEART OF GLASGOW: a Bird's-eye View of Renfield Street, with its Traffic of Trams

74 METROPOLITAN GLASGOW: a Corner of the Shopping Centre

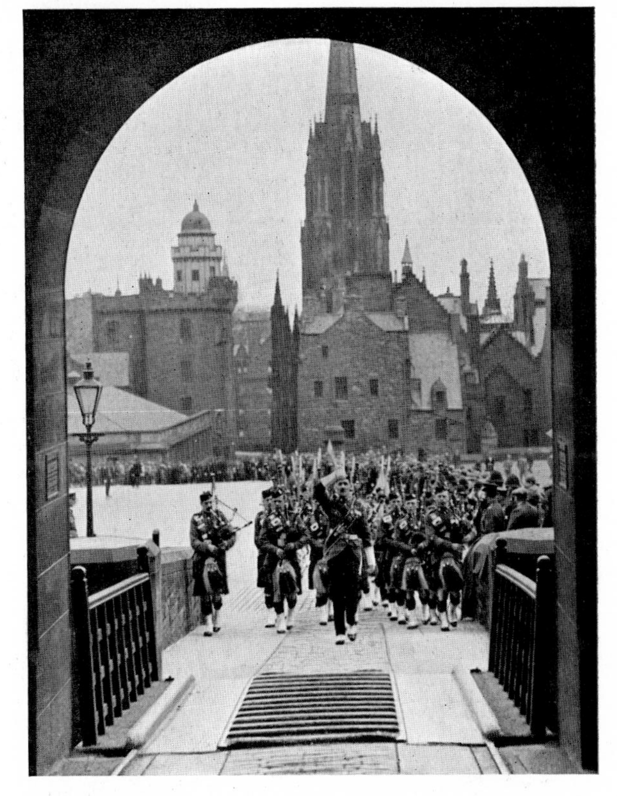

75, 76 ON PARADE! (*Left*) Lenin in George Square, Glasgow, and (*right*) Marching the Colours into Edinburgh Castle

77 GLASGOW : St Vincent Street, with a Glimpse of George Square. The Appropriate Victorian Classicism of the Business Centre

odd results of living where the climate is unreliable, if not so distressing as legend makes it out to be. And a more sombre effect of climatic instability is to be seen, as reinforced by overcrowding, in the low average standard of height among the people, in too many bow-legs and other symptoms of vitamin-deficiency.

Yet it may confidently be maintained that here is the liveliest community in Scotland. This fantastic mixture of racial strains, this collection of survivors from one of the most exacting of social processes, is a dynamo of confident, ruthless, literal energy. The Glasgow man is downright, unpolished, direct, and immediate. He may seem to compare in that respect with the Aberdonian, but in him there is none of that queer Teutonic reserve, which is so apt to affect human intercourse with the native of Buchan. That he is a mighty man with his hands, the world knows and acknowledges; that he is nearer the poet than his brothers in the other cities is less obvious but equally true. He has the "furious" quality of the Scot in its most extreme form. He can be terribly dangerous in revolt and as terribly strong in defence of his own conception of order. He hates pretence, ceremonial, form—and is at the same time capable of the most abysmal sentimentality. He is grave—and one of the world's most devastating sardonic humorists.

This is to look at Glasgow largely in terms of the working man; and that is justified by his predominance in the social scheme of the untidy city of the West. Glasgow's large and respectable bourgeoisie we shall encounter later on, just as we shall see how the generality of Glasgow people manifest themselves in various social directions. It is enough just now to note the large, coarse untidiness of this city by the Clyde, and to observe why there should exist between it and Edinburgh a notorious jealousy. It is common form to regard that jealousy as a joke, but it can be a deadly reality. The graceful capital of tradition must resent this upstart phenomenon of the West, so much richer, so much more practically powerful than itself, so inveterately provincial; and Glasgow in its turn must feel aggrieved that the seats of all formal authority are in the relatively small city of the East that can give itself so many airs and is yet, in the Western view, so unfaithful to the Scottish realities.

The jealousy is as significant as it is real. It symbolises the clash of Teuton and Gael, of the Scotland of tradition and the Scotland of hard and ugly fact. And it is just typical of Scottish life that one of its most dramatic features should be a schism. The race seems to thrive on differences, on contending, in the Stevensonian phrase, "for the shade of a word." Many a good Scots cause has been lost through the absurdities of this inter-city rivalry. It may, in a detached view, have been the accomplished fate of Scotland to lose its soul in niggling quarrels.

In the matter of criticism of Scotland, Lamb's pointed rapier, one may think, was a good deal more deadly than Johnson's elephantine fun at the direct expense of poor, foolish Boswell. There is much in Elia's charges and in those of Sydney Smith. It is not easy dealing with a folk so literal, so eager to do battle on even a metaphysical issue. But we have to reflect at the same time that this characteristic, so awkward, so paralysing to the internal unity of the country, may yet be a symptom of vitality. Curious, indeed, that the tendency should disappear when the Scot goes abroad to fulfil his dreadful destiny of Empire-builder! In his cities and their rivalries he is certainly most true to himself.

78, 79 GLASGOW: the Prim and the Slattern

80 A LOCHSIDE KIRK, GROUPING PLEASANTLY AGAINST THE HILLS AT MENTEITH, PERTHSHIRE

CHAPTER VI

THE KIRK AND THE PEOPLE

He is to be forgiven who, studying the religious history and life of Scotland as a result of realising that intensity of religious experience has been one of the biggest factors in the making of Scotland what it is, finds his subject extremely complex and decidedly comic in many of its aspects.

That the Scots in the main adhere to the Presbyterian system is a generalisation that cannot satisfy anybody who gives the matter some real attention. Fifty years ago the native capacity for schism, as manifested by the numerous subdivisions of the faith into sects, must have seemed baffling to any but the specialist; and it has that power of bewilderment even to this day. The national eccentricity even in the mere matter of ecclesiastical architecture is a thing for eternal wonder—so many styles, from the arid, grudging squareness of Heritor's Gothic to the many unhappy and half-hearted experiments in the adoption of the true Gothic to the northern reserve, testifying remarkably to the uneasiness and significance of this particular experience. On every hand, indeed, there is evidence that Scotland has taken the theological problem with the most intense gravity and the farthest-reaching results.

Is it necessary to say at this late hour that Presbyterianism represents a democratic ideal? It is certainly in essence a denial of the traditional claim of the State to exercise authority in matters of faith. It reserves the essential rights to the worshippers; it gives powers to the Congregation; and it defies the conception of a hierarchy.

That such an ideal has its merits, and that behind such a political façade can flourish the most earnest and beautiful spirit of devotion, only the uncharitable and the foolish would deny. But the fact to be grasped is that, through this insistence on denominational niceties, the

L

Scottish people really expressed their political ideal. It was really very largely an accident that religion became the chopping-block of endless disputes. It was just because the English made one of their few, but in this case lamentable, mistakes by seeking to impose on the Reformed Scots their southern notions of what was right and wrong in the bases and the forms of worship. The numerous and even ludicrous squabbles of denominationalism in Scotland were really the symptoms of political rebellion against the English power. Religion happened to be the Scot's rawest spot.

The tale of this denominationalism is truly fantastic in its details. To go back to the position in the eighteenth century is to invade the realms of the larger lunacy. We find a group that claims to be the true-blue original Church of the Reformation. We find another that, still Presbyterian, holds itself the authentic Church of Scotland through its slightly awkward association with the State. We find that there are secession bodies called Burghers and Anti-Burghers, New Lights and Old Lights; and then proceed to the absurd discovery that there were Old Light Burghers and Old Light Anti-Burghers—and any other apparently fantastic permutation you care to think of. One sect claimed to be Reformed Presbyterian and another, even more boldly, to be the Original Secession. And at a slightly later stage there actually appeared "the Lifters," whose quarrel with the central bodies seems to have developed over a nice dispute as to the manner in which the Elements ought to be raised, in the purely physical sense, from the Communion Table—for there are no Holy Altars in Scotland.

All this ludicrous complexity has now disappeared, but there is Sir James Barrie's testimony that much of the niggling inclination survived into times within human memory; and if "Auld Licht Idylls" is not a masterpiece, it is at least a document. The tendency within Presbyterianism during the last century has all been towards Union—possibly a sign of weakness in

81 A TYPICAL COUNTRY KIRK AT MONZIE, PERTHSHIRE

82 A FINE OLD KIRK INTERIOR AT ABERCORN, WEST LOTHIAN

83 A FISHING VILLAGE IN THE HEBRIDES: Cullipool on the Island of Luing

itself—but no fusion ever takes place without a rump, or even two, being left behind.

One of the more recent and larger events in Scots ecclesiastical history was the Disruption of 1843, when what came to be called the Free Church split from the Church of Scotland on the ancient, sorry issue of patronage. That was an event of the most dramatic order, the recalcitrant ministers sacrificing their livings with a selflessness that must be respected and congregations suffering various, if mild, forms of martyrdom for the sake of a conception of religious liberty.

But even then Scotland had not ended its strange career in the realms of schism. The time arrived, towards the end of last century, when a majority of this Free Church of the Disruption deemed it advisable to unite with the United Presbyterian Church, another schismatic body that had gathered up the odds and ends of the most eccentric eighteenth-century secessions—Old and New Lights, Anti-Burghers and all the rest of them. This famous union was to make the powerful United Free Church—even if it was to produce the notorious and absurd litigation that gave the "Wee Frees" their historical fame and vested in this dour rump the bulk of the funds of the old Free Church proper.

Two points are worth noting in this connection. First of all, the lovely irony of the fact that all rights of patronage had already been removed in 1874 by the Jew, Beaconsfield. And even the present writer can remember the satisfaction in U.P. circles when it was realised that a minor surgical operation, altering U.P. into U.F., would save the expense of a new rubber mat at the door where the elders stood behind the plate—for all the world like tax-gatherers.

Even so, the story was not thus rounded off by any means. There still remained the inevitable, the greatest union of all—that of the authentic Church of Scotland and the United Free Church in 1929. A study of the negotiations leading up to this admirable conclusion

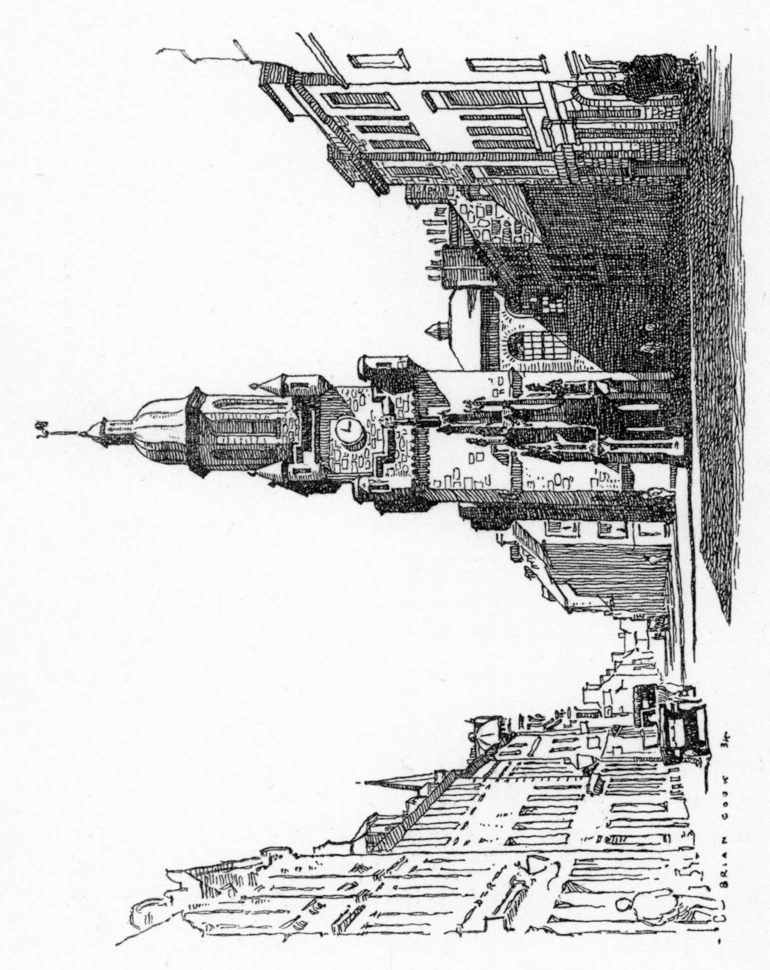

FORRES

would vastly enlighten any serious student of the Scottish character. And it was not, of course, conclusive. The United Free Church left the inevitable rump in the shape of the body that chooses to call itself the United Free Church of Scotland (Continuing), and it flourishes with more ancient remnants to testify to the intensity of theological feeling in Caledonia stern and wild. Let us not forget, at the same time, that such survivals, and the personal sacrifices that invariably go to their achievement, testify also to the existence of something very much finer in the racial mind than a hasty and detached view would suggest.

For that is precisely the point: that all these theological squabbles, narrow and irrelevant as we may think them to be, wonderfully mark the limitations and the possibilities of the Scottish temperament. They have ordained the order of what we can call the Scottish nature in the raw—the tendency to niggle over shades of meaning, the hesitation to accept large generalisations and make easy agreements; the capacity to take pleasures rather cautiously and to look gift-horses in the mouth; the inclination to be literal and not easily humoured; with, on the other hand, the lovely qualities of persistence, industry, thoroughness, accuracy and fidelity.

The blessing has been strangely mixed. Scotland produced at once Peden the Prophet and Sir Andrew Urquhart, the best and most fantastic translator of Rabelais. But if we can begin to comprehend the significance of this superimposition of the capacity to slice metaphysical sausages into the finest slivers on the racial capacity for desperation, we are nearer an understanding of the red heart of Scotland than we could otherwise be.

Scotsmen have really been unhappy victims of circumstance and of the history produced by circumstance. For if this theological complex gave the race some of its most notable qualities, it gave it at the same time an astonishing blindness in those matters of taste and culture and enlightenment that are universally regarded as being the finest that are most legitimately covetable on this sinful earth.

There can be no bones about it: the dullness of Scottish architecture, for instance, is in direct reaction to the ornamentation usually associated with that wicked female, the Whore of Babylon—Rome. The theatre has long been suspect for much the same reasons. Beauty is very generally mistrusted as the manifestation of evil. The ugliness of most of the new Scottish housing schemes can be laid to the charge of those so earnest progenitors who fought against prelatic tyranny—and confused the manifestation with the reality. It is perfectly fair to say that the Reformation, as it shaped in Scotland, wiped out tradition and produced Motherwell as a substitute for Culross. Against the real splendour of the fight for freedom must be set the debits of those numerous things in the Scottish character that are grudging, mean and too literal for average tolerance.

The clouds that occulted the sun of culture (as the mists have always thinned the sunlight that shines rather grudgingly on a relatively barren land) cast their inevitable shadow on the social life of the people. A wet Sunday afternoon in Glasgow is proverbially dull, since, even in a great city, what other races would regard as the most harmless of liberties have been frowned upon. The pervading fear is of licence. The order is one of rigid prohibitions. It is as if the sense of human fallibility haunted the scene. Mistrust governs the situation, and Dora has assuredly a strong Scottish strain in her blood. It might be said that this stringency is not nowadays the will of the people. Be the regulations as austere as you can imagine, the folk contrive to enjoy themselves as well as those who live in countries where there are fewer and easier rules. A purely topical judgment might say, in 1934, that the Scots are rapidly moving towards paganism. But it is at once the fact and the irony and the glory of the situation that this pleasure-loving public of the new age just cannot bring itself to get the rules altered through

84 A LOCHSIDE VILLAGE IN THE HIGHLANDS: a Bird's-eye View of Plockton on Loch Carron

85 SHEEP GRAZING UNDER BEN CRUACHAN, ARGYLL

its beloved channels of democracy. The mere habit of repression is still too strong for it. Still one must keep up appearances.

But all this is not, even so, to be written down too hastily as hypocrisy. It is not so very long ago that the Scots Sabbath was in a majority of households consecrated to nothing but worship. Even as late as the 'eighties of last century the blinds were drawn on Sundays in many households. There was neither cooking of food nor washing of dishes on the Day of Rest, the one duty being discharged on the Saturday, the other left over till the Monday. Even the reading for the day was ordered for the young by stern elders, with *Pilgrim's Progress* marking the limit of licentiousness. One has spoken with members of that generation who remembered the Sundays of their childhood as bleak, grey days when the urgent mind of youth was oppressed by lengthy Church services, interminable sermons, and Bible classes and Sunday schools lasting hours at a time.

It is not, happily, our task to pronounce judgment on the justice or injustice, the wisdom or unwisdom, of such widespread national habits. The fact that they have left abiding marks on Scottish life and character is dramatic enough. Even in the spring of 1934 most of the Presbyteries and many public authorities in the extreme north of the country saw fit to protest before the Traffic Commissioners against the granting of licences to motor-bus companies to run Sunday excursions from the Lowlands into their territories; and when their protests proved in vain, a day of repentance and prayer and humiliation was solemnly and sincerely proposed—and probably observed.

Laughter will not meet such a case. The wise man will salute the consistency and sincerity, even if he think them ill-judged. And always the fact remains that for better or for worse this spirit is at the roots of most Scottish actions and sentiments.

Sentiment is a large part of the make-up of your

average Scot, and it is extremely apt at any moment to slop over into sentimentality—as any student of the performances of Sir Harry Lauder knows how easily he will pass from an exquisite and sharp presentation of a type observed to the most painful yearning for the wee hoose 'mang the heather. That alien and intolerable song, "My Ain Folk," has achieved in Scotland almost the status of a national anthem; and, with a wealth of fine aboriginal minstrelsy at their disposal, too many Scots will know the flush of patriotic feeling on hearing the first, flat-footed chords of Victorian spasms like "Draw the Sword, Scotland!" or swoon in tearful bliss to the emollient strains of that splendid fraud, "Kind, kind, and gentle is she." So also most of the devotion to the memory of Burns—who hated humbug so virulently—is an uncritical indulgence of the emotions, a thoroughly uncultured, if harmless and amusing, falling back on a dim idol and an uneasy loyalty. And, once again, those niggling centuries of denominational concentration must take the blame. For the devotion to bitter sectarism issues distracted the mind of the people from those interests we call cultural, while the positive activities of Presbyterianism in its bad old repressive forms were directly responsible for removing those elements of common life that are at once the results and the inspirations of culture. In that spiritual void, emptied of richness and colour by the sectarians, there was nothing for it but a relapse into the easy ardours of an almost alcoholic sloppiness.

They are all gone into the limbo with that diverting official, the precentor, who lead the praise with tuning-fork and voice in kirks where organs were up till very recent times regarded as suspect "kists o' whustles. . . ." They are all gone, the restrictions, the evasions, the fears of hell fire, the narrow rules. The psychological influence of their long rule remains, and will remain for many generations to come, but the actual performance of the contemporary Scot is little affected by the ancient repressions. There are moments, indeed, when he

DUMFRIES

seems to be heading as fast as possible elsewhere; and the pity of it is that he does not seem at the same time to be escaping from the old restrictions into a particularly healthy region. He is inclined to move towards hedonism, into that strange territory ruled by the spirits of Jazz and the Movies; and it is at least questionable if the advance from an atmosphere which, if uncultured, was at the least disciplined, into one that has no apparent bases of decency at all, can be counted an improvement. This inclination of the popular taste is, Heaven knows, not peculiar to Scotland, but it may be said that, for the reasons stated, it is rather more extensive and extreme in Scotland than elsewhere.

The Church of Scotland, to be sure, is as exquisitely alive to the realities of the situation as any other body of observers. In the spring of 1934 it was responsible for the publication of a report as frank and depressing as its most violent enemy could have desired. This admitted at once that some 36 per cent of the total Scottish population was without any church affiliations whatsoever; while about 150,000 children of school age were not connected with church or even Sunday school. Of the adult population only about 42 per cent adhered in the traditional way to the Kirk; while the number of Roman Catholics in Scotland tended to increase, representing at the time of the report about 13 per cent of the adult population. What the stern great-grandfathers would have said about this state of affairs can only be imagined. Was it for this that they produced the 30,000 volumes of grim theology and nice exegesis that it is the unhappy function of the officials of the Mitchell Library in Glasgow to look after?

The reporting committee took it all very sensibly. It quite soundly traced the causes of the change to movements of population—notably the drift from country to town, the rapid urbanisation of the country, and the Irish immigrations. It concluded that the balance in Scotland as between urban and rural elements is unhealthy and

86 INVERARAY ON LOCH FYNE

87 KELSO, AND RENNIE'S BRIDGE SPANNING THE TWEED

88 LOOKING ACROSS LOCH LINNHE TO BEN NEVIS, WITH FORT WILLIAM AT ITS BASE

requires drastic correction in some way that will check this tendency of the people to become each year less Scottish in blood, tradition and religious attachment.

Yet it is fair enough to say that the Church is somewhat late in the day in facing the Scottish facts, and we may smile ironically to think that, only now, for its own salvation, it is moved to paddle in the main stream of national affairs. It has been complacent these last few decades, itself affected by the very causes it now deplores, and has tended to become rather a strong point of mere social decency than a dynamo of faith. Can it recover its ancient power and once more lead and inspire? That it can never again terrorise its adherents with the fear of Hell Fire is certain.

But the fear of Hell Fire went in the old days with a provocative hatred of the Whore of Babylon, and we may wonder how the thinkers of the Kirk view the rapid growth in stature of that scarlet and interesting woman in their midst. Could the traditional Scotland still be raised on a cry of No Popery?

That is quite possible. The ancient prejudice dies hard. One may imagine, however, that a second Reformation would be inspired much more by the mere débris of prejudice than by burning religious convictions. It is a curiously significant thing that most of the frequent outbreaks of hooliganism and gang-warfare in Glasgow have a quasi-sectarian origin. It is usually Billy and Danny at loggerheads, Orange and Green; but the informed observer will never make the mistake of believing that the fight is ever wholly for a Faith. The organised Churches on both sides are as much concerned with these lively ebullitions of bottle-throwing and razor-slashing as the police. They are really social and racial manifestations—when they do not represent simply rivalry in sport, as in the implacable enmity of the respective supporters of two of Scotland's most famous football clubs: the Glasgow Rangers and the Celtic. Even the teams when they meet do not take the occasion lightly; and it is now common form at such engagements for the police to herd the Rangers' supporters at one end of the field and those of the Celtic at the other, with a battalion of outsized constables continuously marching with solemn but wary tread round the actual arena of play. In such cases, in fact, the root-causes of trouble are to be found in that inveterate wildness of the Scot, which seizes on any excuse for violent schism and can all too easily degenerate into a mere destructive hooliganism.

How great the responsibility of the Kirk for that propensity in the submerged tenth of the Scottish population it would be difficult—and quite unfair to attempt—to say, but the fact of hooliganism may be conveniently considered at this stage. It exists in a particularly grim form north of the Tweed in the industrial areas, and particularly where the Scots-Presbyterian and Irish-Roman elements are intimately mixed; and it has always existed in the populous areas, even before economic depression encouraged its periodical outbreaks in the obvious ways.

It is not simply that bands of wild lads love to lay into each other with substantial weapons from time to time. Far more distressing is the fact that communal property is less safe in Scotland than elsewhere. It is necessary in municipal parks to order the citizens to "keep off the grass," and to enforce the order with rigour. A queer delight in destruction informs too many of the young Scot's activities. He is strangely given to the smashing of street-lamps, the breaking-up of seats on favourite walks, and the violent chalking of walls. And if we can understand it all in relation to the racial and social history of the race, it yet remains one of the most puzzling and disheartening of the facts that go to make up the Scottish paradox.

The element of hooliganism, however, is small in proportion to the noise it makes, and it is not to be regarded as a problem beyond the various authorities. More than one hard-working minister of a slum parish has proved that this rebellious tendency can be easily enough canalised towards useful, or at least peaceful, ends. The larger problem is that represented by those young people of Scotland who belong frankly to the "churchless million" and have an attitude to the Establishment that is one of complete indifference when it is not positively contemptuous.

These are folk who notably abide by the civil law. They are temperate, healthy and keen. Their swing away from formal religion takes the shape of Sunday exercise on foot or awheel, so that all the main roads and hillsides beyond the walls of the larger Scottish towns are thick on the Sabbath day with boisterous young people in bright and scanty costumes. (It is notable, in fact, that the "hikers" of Scotland are given to a more polychromatic style of dress than their brethren in the South.) Almost day by day the rearguard of the Kirk has to suffer defeat on some such question as Sunday golf. Even that sturdy pillar of Sunday Observance, the middle class, has discovered that a run in the car after morning service seems to have no temporal consequences; and the fact that it indulges itself thus shows that the ancient fear of fire and brimstone in the Hereafter is a thing of the past.

Gallantly the Church seeks to accommodate itself to the new conditions. Ministers have been heard to defend in open Presbytery, eloquently and with sense, the Sunday golfing proclivities of their parishioners. More than one, seeing the weekly efflux from the town and realising its importance (if not its significance), has opened the doors of his church at an early hour so that those numerous pilgrims of the open spaces may worship if they care.

No experiment of the kind has been successful in full. And why should it? The tedious order of morning service at eleven, evening at six-thirty—with the churches locked and barred through the week—has created a habit where there might have been a glowing impulse.

Well may we ask: What of those eager youngsters

who are moving about the countryside as they would not have dared to do in the early years of King George's reign? If they have renounced the Kirk of their fathers, are they discovering some new vision of their native land?

LINLITHGOW CHURCH AND GATEWAY TO PALACE

89 CHOPPY WEATHER IN THE KYLES OF BUTE

90 SHEEP-DIPPING IN THE HEBRIDES IN ROCK POOLS
AFTER THE RAIN

CHAPTER VII

THE FIRESIDE CLIME

To make a happy fireside clime
To weans and wife;
That's the true pathos and sublime
Of human life.

It may be feared that Robert Burns, poor lad, did not notably achieve the admirable ideal thus expressed in his rhymed epistle to Dr. Blacklock, but he discharged in these lines the poet's sole duty of speaking the authentic voice of his race. Scottish life does centre to a remarkable extent round the hearth and home; the Scottish heart still beats most warmly in the domestic glow. It is a race domesticated quite beyond the ordinary, whether it dwells in the Highland croft-house and takes its chief delight in the *ceilidh*, or in the top flat of a Glasgow tenement and is happy when the relations come in of an evening to exchange the family gossip and make up a table or two of whist.

Of this racial inclination most of the obvious explanations have already been discussed. The climate played its part, of course, but the influence of organised religion in its Scottish forms was all against the development of those communal forms of recreation that other European peoples take quite for granted. The restaurant, the park of the type of Kensington Gardens or the Bois de Boulogne and, least of all, the popular café had little chance of developing until a relatively recent date. One can remember the friends of boyhood, only thirty years ago, who were forbidden the theatre, even the Christmas pantomime, on the basis of the ancient prejudice against the sinful playhouse; and that even although their parents were in no other way conspicuous for narrowness or inhospitality. One even remembers when the word "theatre" on the hand-written bill announcing a boyish production of dolls within the four walls of a converted sugar-box had to be altered to "entertainment."

This was quite directly the influence of the Kirk; though the apprehension was strangely mingled with a purely social fear of "what the neighbours would say." It is not an attitude that has survived the War in any degree worth mentioning. Yet the fact remains that the social life of Scotland, especially among the extensive middle classes, is based to a remarkably large extent on Church associations. If this cannot be credited to the Kirk as a triumph of burning faith, it is a considerable achievement in the way of influence, nevertheless.

A great number of households look to congregational associations to provide the richest of their recreative opportunities. The congregation must always have its "socials," at which minister and flock mingle in a pleasant atmosphere of jocularity, tea and music. The Bible class and the Sunday school have their characteristic and frequent jollifications—certainly the "soireé" (or "swarry") in winter and the "trip" in summer. The Dorcas Meeting allows the womenfolk to forgather and chat over the afternoon biscuits. Lantern lectures and mid-week prayer meetings continue the chain of intercourse. And even the choir practice, with its distinguished opportunities for the meeting of the sexes, serves its very large part in the establishment of continuity and solidity in church life.

It is the easiest thing in the world to laugh at these ebullitions and satirise them. By metropolitan standards they have undoubtedly their appearance of the ludicrous and the dismally respectable. But let us remember our values and realise that the home-keeping qualities, if dull and unpretentious, tending to the replacement of intelligence by sentimentality, are yet lovely virtues, and that country is happy which, like Scotland, has a large section of its inhabitants resolutely devoted to them. There is to be found among this people degrees of plain worth, of warm hospitality, and unaffected decency such as few nations of the earth can rival; and all the understandable

91 A TYPICAL CROFTING TOWNSHIP AT ARDVASSAR, SKYE

92, 93 NEW AND OLD: the Hand Loom and the Wireless Set in the Hebrides

squeals of the young intellectuals of the new age against a colourless bourgeoisie cannot deprive that fact of its value.

It would be quite misleading to suggest that all this intensity of domesticity is traceable to the religious influence. As before, the climate, the relative poverty of the land and its emptiness before the industrial concentration encouraged the quiet habit of living. The institution of the family throve in such conditions, and it is round the family standard that your average Scot still rallies most readily. It is not without meaning that few peoples have such an abiding interest in genealogy and take such delight in recalling and unravelling tangles of relationship—who was "married on" whom, precisely the year of Jock's departure for Queensland, and all the kindly little turns of the family fortune. The generations seem to hang together more closely than they do elsewhere, so that aunts and uncles, cousins, nephews, nieces and all the in-laws share a tribal interest. It is a matriarchal system in the main. It thrives on cosy gossip. The neighbours are fair game; even their washings, so conspicuous under the tenement system, being held as evidence against them. And a stranger, privileged somehow to listen-in to a family colloquy, would assuredly be impressed by the vast, almost luxurious, interest taken in the details of illness and death: the national mind running with curious delight along sombre lines.

That stranger in any Scottish town would receive at first a strong impression of inhospitality, but it is quite misleading. The Scotsman does not readily offer the freedom of the home to the alien. That is partly honest shyness. It is partly, though in a very small degree, the native caution. But it is mainly a deference to the authority of the woman in the home. The woman must be consulted and given the opportunity to make preparation for reception on an impressive scale. She is house-proud, and she dislikes being caught *en pantoufles*. And that recognition of her supreme domestic authority reveals, as it happens, a somewhat uneasy balance in the social life of Scotland. For if the wife rules in her own drawing-room—or parlour or kitchen—she is not readily admitted to a share of the masculine adventures beyond the home. There is still a curious segregation of the sexes in the social field. The organisation of Scottish society is still to that extent quaintly primitive.

Barriers down, however, it is our privilege then to encounter that unique, that noble Scottish institution—the High Tea; which is the very best that the Scots housewife of the average sort can do for you within the home. The native still takes his dinner in the middle of the day. To eat dinner in the evening, especially to mention the fact, is to be suspected of either eccentricity or pretentiousness. Afternoon tea is either a feminine indulgence or an English fad. The true glory resides in that fine, confused meal of the evening, when the board groans under at least one dish of a solid order—meat or fish or eggs or whatnot—when all the products of the bakery are available in fantastic profusion, and when every hesitation on the part of the satiated visitor is covered with the offer of still another cup of rather strong Indian tea. Even Englishmen have been known to talk in fondly reminiscent mood of orgies of the kind, and it can be said that, particularly for one who has worked or played long in the open air—which is precisely the sort of person for whose benefit it was no doubt devised—it holds many and curious satisfactions: especially if the woman of the house has properly relied mainly on the peculiarly native dishes.

This is no place for a discourse on the merits of the Scots Kitchen. The curious will find all that can be said about it in Miss Marian McNeill's charming compilation of that name. Nor can we say that the Scotswoman of to-day is distinguished as a good cook in any cosmopolitan sense. It may be feared that she has forgotten a great deal of the traditional skill in that direction. She has anything but ready access to the ingredients so

94, 95 HIGHLAND INDUSTRIES: (*above*) Netting Salmon on the Tay; (*below*) Collecting Peats in Barra, Outer Hebrides

96, 97 PRIMITIVE SOUTH UIST: (*above*) the Use of the *Cas-Chrom*, or Hand Plough; (*below*) Cutting Peats

easily available to the woman keeping house in, say, London. (Greengrocers in the Scottish towns are apt to exhibit beside the bundles recipes for the cooking of it when they display asparagus in their windows—as if it were some queer, exotic vegetable.) She is not catering for people with sophisticated palates. So, if she is a good cook, she is as likely as not to be in the class of good, plain cook; that plainness being as much a feature of her performance as the goodness.

But there yet remains one culinary direction in which the Scot is utterly *hors concours*, with only the Belgian offering any substantial rivalry. In bakery the race excels. There are few travellers who have not been ravished by the simplest native efforts in this direction—by the sweet, clean goodness of girdle scones, by the crisp and exquisite oatcakes, by the golden savours of pancakes, and the dry charm of good shortbread: those delights that in every decent hotel await the climber off the hill or the fisher from the burn.

It may be feared that in the towns the art has declined, but that is only because in its commercialised forms the bakery of Scotland yet remains superb. Edinburgh and Glasgow give the world its most delicious biscuits. The fascias of shops in Hampstead and Chelsea given over to this sort of commerce bear proudly the adjective "Scotch." Such thoroughfares as Union Street, Glasgow, and Princes Street, Edinburgh, seem sometimes like bazaars organised to the greater glory of the craft. Here is wealth of attraction: such a display of sheer cereal goodness in every conceivable form that one is driven to visualise a nation with a sweet tooth and somewhat dubious dietetic standards; though a memory of the national significance of the High Tea should help us to an understanding of the phenomenon.

That the art has been so extensively, though so splendidly, commercialised is significant. We have seen how a Highland community will rely for its supply of bread on distant Glasgow. We have to understand that, except for a handful of cottager-women here and there, the reliance among the working people is largely on the multiple store and the can. Such is one of the prices of intensive industrialism. There is authority for saying that in Glasgow the labouring man's wife rarely carries her culinary adventures beyond the frying of sausages. Those qualified to judge declare that she has almost entirely lost the sense of true domestic economy. The stock-pot is an institution unknown or forgotten, and there is nothing left of the fine French sense of saving to-day's scrap for to-morrow's tit-bit. The point is topical, but observers have anxiously noted how, as a result of widespread industrial depression, the womenfolk of the crowded areas, rid of the necessity to get a well-fed man out to his work at an early hour of the morning, have rapidly declined in this matter of domestic decency. Who would blame them for that? one may well ask, realising the bitterness of their situation. But the point is worth making as emphasising the fate of a Scotland too much overlaid by industrialism at the best.

The largeness of this rough industrial element, as against the tenacity with which the bourgeoisie sticks to its respectability, renders the task of generalisation both difficult and unsafe, but certain common customs are worth noting. Over most of the country, for instance, July is the chosen holiday month, the Glasgow Fair—as who should say Wakes—usually spanning the second and third weeks of it. In a country so small and so fiercely indented by the besieging sea, the holiday drive is largely towards "the Coast," the Glasgow million having at its command the many amenities and peerless beauty of the Firth of Clyde. To go "doon the watter" is conventional, the family of any substance taking its villa for the month at one of the remarkably quiet and sweet resorts of that vast estuary, the people crowding to such popular resorts as Dunoon, Rothesay, Largs and Saltcoats, and there living for the most part in conditions of gregariousness that would only with difficulty pass the municipal authorities at home. Wherever they go, however, the Scots still go mainly in the family group. All the latterday facilities for travelling may have affected them, and the motor-vehicle has vastly increased the range of adventure, but the fireside remains the dominant symbol. Few Scottish hotels could live on the natives of the land alone.

Yet another feature of the communal life that must impress the stranger is the devotion of the housewife to washing. The Scotswoman may not be one of the world's great cooks, but only in Holland does one encounter a passion like hers for scrubbed floors, spotless stairs, and garments and bedware exhaustively washed and bleached. In most households the "washing day" is the one of the week when men tread warily in the domestic preserves and the rhythm of domestic affairs moves in accordance with the performance of a worn woman with blenched fingers, hired to bend over the tubs. The city houses may not have gardens, but each has some sort of space for the drying of clothes outdoors, so that the gay bunting of a family washing is one of the most characteristic features of the Scottish streetscape. Each tall tenement has its "green," and rigid is the law governing the order of its use and of that of the wash-house key, and fiercely contested is any infringement of the unwritten law.

It is almost stirring to see how the wives of the miners have a peculiar regard for this approximation to godliness. They seem always to be at the tub, and there is a queer contrast between the hovels in which too many of them live and the loving care with which decent garments are hung out to flutter in the westerly wind and the harsh overalls of the pit, scrubbed religiously, pegged to dry by the low doors. The little washings hanging from the poles that project from the high windows of "the lands" are a very characteristic feature of the Edinburgh scene—providing warrant for the charming story of the country minister who, late for some meeting during Assembly Week, explained that he had been perambulating the High Street, studying "the short and simple flannels of the poor."

A score of customs, or inclinations, of the kind could be advanced in support of the main suggestion that the social life of Scotland is relatively simple in its structure and pretensions, securely based on the institution of the family. But once we have agreed upon that, we have to attempt to square it with the fact, quite ineluctable, that the Scots are a race of heavy drinkers. It may be that their actual indulgences are no more numerous than those of, say, the English or the French or the Germans, but it is just beyond argument—there are yards of statistics to prove it—that they are more given to drunkenness.

Now, this concern does not take us so far from the fireside clime as might appear at first sight. It is as good a clue to the true nature of the race as the female passion for washing and scrubbing. It harks back, in fact, to the feature already noted: the uneasy mixing of the sexes in affairs outwith the home.

If the woman rules by the fireside, the man is the devil of a fellow in the outer world. France and, to a lesser extent, England achieve reasonable temperance precisely because the pleasures of drinking are shared and openly indulged. In Scotland it is quite otherwise. There may be not a drop of drink in the true drunkard's household. The drunkard is likely to know shame on being seen to enter a public-house. Women patronising public places of refreshment in Scotland are immediately suspect, and in houses of any pretensions it will sometimes be clearly indicated that their presence is unwelcome. "This is for men only," says the unwritten law; and it is all—like so many other absurdities and hypocrisies one could so easily detail—the product of that repression which accompanied the Presbyterian revolt. It is a natural instinct driven underground, its indulgences rendered furtive. If the student would know to what preposterous lengths an administration may have to go in order to

98, 99 WOMEN MUST WORK—IN THE OUTER ISLES

100, 101 THE HERRING CATCH: Sorting and Packing the Fish at Castlebay, Barra

compromise between public convenience and the force of convention, he need only study the regulations whereby refreshment is obtainable on Sundays in Scotland only by the registered hotel-patron or the *bona fide* traveller—an abstraction the Law has been hard put to it within recent years to define.

Here is assuredly Scotland's most flamboyant hypocrisy. But the politics of such matters cannot concern us in this particular inquiry, and the Law would probably not be such an ass in these matters if the race were naturally sober. The existence in the North of a very active and powerful temperance movement is not just a symptom of narrowness, inept as its methods may seem to us to be. It was only to Scotland that a British Government dared to apply an Act providing for Local Option in the matter of licences; and it is beside the point that the experiment was a ludicrous failure, and that the Act is a dead letter to all intents and purposes. A general proclivity produced these phenomena, and it has to be reckoned with and accounted for.

The explanation of it is assuredly not in the fact that whisky is a native product. Whisky is an admirable beverage when sensibly used, and the Scot has no easier access to it than the Englishman. (As it happens, the appropriate references in literature suggest that ale was once as definitely the drink of the people as it still is in England.) What we have to determine are the causes of an admittedly excessive devotion to the more potent liquor, and surely they are obvious. Life in a hard land with an unfriendly climate creates an almost physiological need for fierce stimulants. The "furious" quality of the racial strain inclines a man to desperate measures. But it is perhaps just enough to say that the living conditions almost anywhere in the industrial belt are quite enough to drive any man to drink.

Any Lanarkshire steel-worker will strangely enlighten the curious as to the capacity of the human frame in its Scottish form for the absorption of strong drink. One has heard a man of the old school—and confirmed his claim—tell how a half-bottle of whisky was his customary ration before breakfast in the brave days of his physical prime and of regular employment in the rolling-mills, and how any man of his kind, making good money at the most gruelling of all occupations, would consume the best part of two bottles of whisky in a day, with many pints of beer thrown in by way of decorative embroidery. The conventional refreshment of the working man in the industrial belt is still "a half and half-pint" or, doubling the dose, "a glass and a chaser"—that is, a glass of neat whisky washed down by a pint of beer. The Scots "glass," by the way, is a larger measure than the English "double" and the Scots ale heavier than the Sassunach bitter.

How shall we explain it all? Climate, strength and the heavy nature of industrial work do not take us quite far enough. Surely it is all produced by a combination of these elements with, above them all, the sheer need to escape, by whatever means, from an almost intolerable environment.

The worst days are over. All sorts of factors—notably better housing conditions and the belated discovery of ways of escape from the drab towns—are working a slow but steady revolution in the drinking habits of the people. Much rests on the outcome of certain evolutionary processes that wear, at the moment of writing, a purely topical air. Everything, in fact, depends on Scotland's economic future. Have her heavy industries declined beyond the possibility of recovery to the 1914 standard? Will she ever regain stability, her population distributed with some approximation to sanity?

All that remains now is to praise the late Miss Cranston. . . . Miss Cranston—she died at the age of 85 early in 1934—was a native of Glasgow. Early in life she conceived the idea that the man of affairs in that great and growing city would welcome the institution of restaurants in which he could be sure of a good, cheap lunch and

102 THE FRIENDLY HIGHLAND INN: a Typical Example in Wild Surroundings at Kingshouse, by the Entrance to Glencoe, with Buchaille Etive beyond

103 WHISKY : a Solemn Business at a Distillery

count on a decent cup of tea or coffee when he felt so inclined.

It was a remarkably intelligent anticipation of a great social development. Glasgow was growing rapidly. A return to the suburban home in the middle of the day was becoming a physical impossibility for the ordinary man of business. It was manifest that he would not be willing to spend too much good money on his sustenance. Hence, in the long run, Miss Cranston's chain of tea-rooms that made Scottish history and encouraged, ultimately, the coffee habit among the wearers of the bowler hat. There is no business visitor to a Scottish city who has not heard the reception clerk say of his, or her, principal: "Oh, he's gone out for a coffee"; few who have not transacted affairs over that innocent beverage—while men now not yet so very old will tell you how, in the bad old days, business was not business in Glasgow unless conducted "over a dram."

That was Miss Cranston's achievement. Her example has been universally copied; it has universally triumphed. And it is a peculiarly jolly fact that this wonderful old lady enlisted in her service the best architects and decorative artists she could lay hands on. That is why the patrons of her most successful successor and rival may enjoy, for the price of a cup of coffee, the contemplation of the pictures the best artists of the Glasgow School could produce. She very nearly worked a miracle with this shrewd and intelligent combination of industry and art; and when the perfect history of Scotland comes to be written her name will not be omitted.

A nation of whisky-drinkers; a nation of coffee-drinkers. . . . But it is just the old paradox all over again. We are dealing with a queer and queerly circumstanced people.

CHAPTER VIII

A NOTE ON SPORT

The old allegation, that they take their pleasures sadly, was levelled against the English people in particular; and, by Continental standards, the Scots must share the charge. But there is just that about the recreative behaviour of the Northern people that justifies one in saying that they are much more apt than the English to take their pleasures madly. A hundred thousand fanatics cheering an International football team to victory in the great bowl of Hampden Park, Glasgow—even the smaller band that urges a Scottish Rugby XV at Murrayfield to desperate deeds with the war-cry of "Feet, Scotland, feet!"—suggests a dark and vehement passion of interest far transcending in intensity the light-hearted clamour of an English crowd at Wembley or Twickenham.

Football is Scotland's game, and infinitely more representative than golf. Indeed, a large number of illusions about the sporting proclivities of the race have now to be shattered. It is true that golf, for instance, is a more truly democratic game in Scotland than in England. Notably in Fife and Ayrshire, the artisan has an easy and traditional access to his local links. But to believe that every Scottish child can swing a club at the moment of escape from the cradle is an absurdity of legend. Whatever may have been the case in the past, the game is as elsewhere largely the affectation of the upper and middle classes and a fashionable form of escape from the exigencies of city life. It is really not an interest of the country as a whole.

That it should elsewhere be regarded as Scotland's ruling passion is actually a curiously suggestive illustration of the way in which the country has come to be regarded more as a picturesque playground than as an economic and social reality. The same sort of misappre-

104 FOOTBALL IN SCOTLAND: the Crowd on "International Day" at Hampden Park, Glasgow

105 THE RULING PASSION: Queues of Football Enthusiasts for the "International" at Hampden Park, Glasgow

hension—one had almost said sentimentality—attributes an infinitely greater importance than they possess to Highland Games, with esoteric pursuits like tossing the caber, putting the weight, and dancing the Highland Fling as high-lights of the "quaint" and semi-barbaric performance.

Highland Games are largely a Victorian and English invention. They are an emanation of that spirit so admirably nicknamed "Balmorality" by Mr. George Scott-Moncrieff. The good Queen Victoria must be held responsible for them. That marvellous lady so took the Highlands to her capacious heart, so delighted in the thin Stuart strain in her blood, and found so much romance in the symbolic figure of John Brown, that her taste, backed by the Royal authority, imposed on the Highlands this spectacular, Anglo-German fraud.

What Scottish reality could there possibly be in a highly organised affair, staged almost entirely for the benefit of alien landowners, who offer to Scotland the last insult of the assumption of the kilt and are in Scotland only to have so many acres of it all to themselves? Such people, mere victims of fashion though they may be, are wounds in the heart of Scotland—and the bitterness of it is that, except with a very few honourable exceptions, the presence of a handful of nominally genuine native aristocrats does not mitigate the unreality of these gatherings. They, too, have been shaped by such influences as Eton, Sandhurst, the Guards and London in the Season, and they are only extensions of the alien stain on the domestic scene. A few pretty pictures in the *Tatler* do not give the crofter a decent bit of land or the ordinary traveller access to mountains.

The Highlander accepts it all? He does; and it can be acknowledged that the spectacle of his evasive deference to, let us say, an American plutocrat is not a pretty one. We may reflect, however, that it was for a loyalty his spirit was broken. Absurd as the transition from sport to politics may seem, the terms of the various Acts

ST. ANDREWS

designed to suppress the warlike proclivities of the Highlander—after the Jacobite Rebellions—bear directly on these queer displays we are discussing. These were surely the most ferocious enactments ever conceived. Intended to reduce the Highlander's inclination to war, they simultaneously and inevitably reduced him to the condition of a serf. Once again, Scotland is not understood until the terms of these Acts are considered and appreciated in all their cruelty.

To return to the Games, however, it can be acknowledged that severe tests of physical strength such as tossing the caber, throwing the hammer, and so forth are in the true Highland tradition, even if they wear nowadays the air of artificial revivals. There is no doubt at all that the Highlander does take delight in the Gatherings, especially in those events that are confined to the natives of the given district, in the piping, and in the dancing.

It remains the deplorable, the ludicrous, fact that these fashionable occasions mainly provide a happy hunting-ground for peripatetic pot-hunters, largely from the Lowlands, who go round in a solid group from fixture to fixture, as gipsies move from fair to fair, and exhibit themselves day after day during the season to make the Roman holiday. (It is even whispered that discreet "arrangements" among the regular performers are not uncommon.) So with the pipers to a large extent; and so also with those feat little dancers who are certainly a delight to the eye. They are mainly professionals from the Lowlands, the offspring of colliers and such, trained like whippets for the job, trailed from centre to centre by eager mothers, and treated very much like valuable pedigree livestock. The Games, in fact, have very little validity as expressions of the native taste in play.

Where he has not entirely succumbed to the lure of football, the game that seems to come most natural to the Highlander is shinty. This lively pastime might be called hockey in the rough, with no nonsense about "sticks" and rules of a relatively free and easy kind. It bears the stamp of an aboriginal game, the sort of game that village boys might improvise with crooked boughs and a knot of wood on the common land in the evening. Now it produces representative teams in all sorts of improbable places throughout the North and West. There is something like a League; there is at least a Cup; and a good deal has latterly been done towards effecting a competitive compromise with exponents of the kindred Irish game of hurling. It is certainly one of the most dashing and truly natural of native games; and a typical crowd at a good shinty match is as eager and representative a group as the outraged Highlands can nowadays produce.

The Scots have several odd and distinctive devotions of the kind. Thus, in the industrial districts, the wayfarer will come on a Saturday afternoon upon a group of sombrely clad men, intent on watching others throw bright rings of steel through the air to land as near as possible to scraps of paper set into squares of muddy clay. This game of quoits is probably not indigenous, but it is a distinctively Scottish passion, and again the apparatus of leagues, championships and challenge matches encourages its survival. Here the local rivalries are keen; it is a game played sternly and often for money; and few things are more characteristic, more pathetically characteristic, of the industrial scene than the shabby little alleys, grassless and grim, in which collier and steel-worker fight their battles with the whirling hoops of metal.

Indeed, the industrial population has a whole range of recreative interests all its own, and it is perhaps reaction in its simplest form that governs the association of so many of them with birds and beasts. Thus the homing-pigeon must sublimate for many a Lanarkshire miner the instinct of escape, just as the extensive interest in the breeding of cage-birds is but a means of return to the good soil, even if the circumstances of the taking and keeping of lark and linnet sometimes fall short of the

106 TYPICAL SCENE AT THE BRAEMAR GATHERING

107 THE ROARING GAME: Curlers on a Moorland Loch in Lanarkshire

humane ideal. So it is also common to see the collier with a lean whippet at heel, though it is said that the vogue of greyhound-racing has considerably affected this particular fancy. The thrill of the gamble is apparently a good enough substitute for the excitements of poaching.

The art of curling vies with golf as a Scottish legend, and where and when it is possible it has those eminently democratic features conventionally attributed to it: laird and small tenant forgetting the social distinctions in the rigour of the roaring game. Unhappily, the opportunities are rare enough in natural conditions. Rural depopulation proceeds apace; the native gentry inclines more and more to infidelity; and the Scottish climate is not so bitter in winter as legend would have us believe. The opening of ice-rinks in the cities has given the game a new sort of popularity, but in such conditions it loses, one fears, its aboriginal savours. Nevertheless, at least one Scotsman still makes his living by fashioning curling-stones from the granite of Ailsa Craig.

On the whole, however, it may be said that the Scots differ very little from their neighbours in their recreative tastes, except in the matter of the intensity with which they approach their pastimes. Is it characteristic of them that they are mighty gamblers?

It does not square with the legend of the canny Scot, but all the evidence goes to show that they are plungers of an inveterate and desperate sort. On every hand the working man is to be heard anxiously debating the possible outcome of horse-races to be run four hundred miles away. His literature consists very largely of books of form, special sporting editions of the newspapers, and those frequent afternoon issues of the evening sheets that are only justified by the arrival of results from distant Epsom or Newbury. They are a people who have few opportunities for ever seeing a horse-race. Meetings in Scotland are rare and of very minor importance—Ayr, Musselburgh and Hamilton being the most famous of the surviving gatherings. Yet that this passion for betting affects the mass of the population is beyond a doubt. It is inextricably bound up with the genuine passion for football as an art. It is probably the biggest social problem of post-War Scotland.

When we mention football we come into the realms of the national obsession. We can say, if we please, and with a good deal of truth, that the game is vilely commercialised. We may think it absurd that a local sentiment should be focussed on a team of hirelings, probably not one of them with a local association, all subject to being bought and sold like so many white slaves. But we make a vast mistake if—allowing for all that, and admitting that the enthusiasm is closely bound up with the excitements of betting on results—we do not realise that the devotion is still something in the nature of a culture.

There is excellent warrant for regarding Scotland as the birthplace of football. Historical references to the game are ancient and numerous, and it is even on record that Mary, Queen of Scots, had her mind taken off the anxieties of the Battle of Langside by a game played by her retainers. And surely it can fairly be suggested that the passion of partisanship is really a recompense for something lost—perhaps for the clan system and the tribal battles finally wiped out by the vicious Acts of suppression already mentioned. There are so few other loyalties to which the industrial population may sincerely adhere.

However that may be, the national expertise in football, the excessive interest in it apart, is immense. The crowds that flock to the Saturday afternoon matches in their tens of thousands are *cognoscenti* to a man. They will know the football history of every player on the field. Individual performances will be carefully studied and judiciously assessed. Not a decision of the referee but will be the subject of extremely violent but fully enlightened comment. A glamour of classicism has been thrown over the bull-fights of Spain, and the Andalusian hordes are credited by the romanticists with a pretty taste in the

108 THE ROYAL AND ANCIENT GAME: the Famous Links at North Berwick, with the Bass Rock beyond

109 OUT FOR SALMON ON THE TUMMEL RIVER, PERTHSHIRE

technique of cattle-slaughter. They are assuredly no more wise in their native art than the Scot in his judgment of the aboriginal game. A crowd at Hampden Park—and 130,000 people have gathered before this on those stark terraces at one time—is a gathering of schoolmen. Be their arguments as rough as you please, their language such as would appal the Common Room of All Souls, the controversies are yet conducted with a true gravity, a fine feeling for values, and an abounding delight in skill that even partisanship cannot mitigate.

But the feature of a great Scottish football occasion that must surprise and even alarm the stranger is the intensity of the passion engendered. The roar of a Glasgow crowd at Cup Final or International is a thing never to be forgotten—so strong, so vehement, so feral is it. The dour and silent Scot of legend has disappeared, and in his place there stands, on his tiptoes, a wild thing gone berserk with enthusiasm and rage. To stand among the perfervid on the terraces of say, Celtic Park, is to receive the most liberal education in the nuances of obscenity available in our modern world. It is to be among a wild, strong, desperate, ebullient people. It is to see the Scot in the natural state. It is to enjoy a sight of him, without which no understanding of what he really is could be called complete.

And football has all the commonalty of Scotland in its thrall. Every little village of the rural Lowlands has its team and its loyalty. When you see goalposts set in a field on the outskirts of a Highland hamlet, do not be too sure that the local game is shinty. One has even seen, in a fishing hamlet of the Hebrides, how an enterprising boy may make pocket-money by selling written slips of football results, noted down from the wireless, in places where men congregate.

This eagerness for news of the game is undoubtedly related to the craze for betting on results. The Scottish working-man spends a lot of his time, and probably too much of his money, in filling up on Friday evenings what he calls his "coupoon." This coupon is simply a bettir slip, offering the expert a variety of odds for a varie of forecasts, and the weekly completion of it is a ma of the most anxious deliberation. The "pool" is a r modern variant of the same old gamble. In this cas bookmaker issues a selection of fixtures, both Sc and English, and generously offers to divide the w subject to certain crafty deductions, among those forecast correctly, or to within an error or two, t results of the games set forth on his alluring sheet. As for the "accumulator" and other agreeable means of getting rich quickly, their nature can be imagined. It is enough to say that speculation of this type amounts in Scotland to a fever.

The morality of the business is beside the point in our inquiry. All we have to reckon with is the fact that the true sporting proclivities of the Scottish people do not notably include the shooting of grouse, the stalking of deer, or even the chasing of the wee gutta ba': those charming pursuits attributed to them by sentiment. We are simply discovering once more, at the end of this line of inquiry, further proof of the excessive urbanisation of the people.

It is not, indeed, in their sports that the Scots are any longer unique; it is in the way, the mad, wild way, they take them. They are urbanised to the standard modern pattern. And yet that queer element of the inveterate Scottishness—if we could only define it!—remains to mark them as a race apart.

110, 111 TRADITION IN ARCHITECTURE: (*above*) Kirkpatrick Kirk, Dumfries; (*below*) Barcaldine Castle, Argyllshire

112, 113 CLASSIC AND BARONIAL IN A COUNTRY SETTING: (*above*) Gosford House, Haddingtonshire, and (*below*) Glamis Castle, Forfar

CHAPTER IX

INSTITUTIONS, LEGENDS AND REALITIES

It is not yet possible for any man to attempt a detached survey of this queer country of Scotland without incurring a considerable number of risks. He is in danger always of disappointing those foreigners who find delight in the land north of the Tweed almost entirely on account of superlative scenery and an astonishing wealth of romantic association. He is almost certain to infuriate that vast body of Scots which, living in circumstances almost indistinguishable from those that prevail in Manchester or Birmingham, remains largely under the spell of Walter Scott and believes, or tries to believe, that Glasgow and Dundee have somehow, by virtue of some indefinable racial quality, a romantic advantage over the English cities. He is liable to be suspected on both sides of a wilful adventure in the gentle modern art of "debunking."

Something has already been said of the besetting Scots sin of sentimentality, but has enough been said to make it clear that the conventional idolisation of Robert Burns is one of its most understandable and least important phases? There is in the Scottish mind an unwillingness, amounting almost to an insincerity, to face the facts bearing on the state of the Scottish heart. The past was so glorious. "Here's tae us! Wha's like us?"—and let the facts, and the plain deductions from the facts, be forgotten. It would be idle to suggest that the Scot of to-day is easy in his mind as to the true state of his highly industrialised country. He must know that the memory of Bonnie Prince Charlie, charming as it is, has no bearing on the condition of Bellshill, and that the loveliness of Morar does not compensate for the subsidised pauperisation of its crofters. But from his very uneasiness he flies all the more gladly to the illusions. He is a man suffering from

people. It is more truly a characteristic creation of the people—expressing, as it happens, some of their very best qualities. It is grave, exact and just. And otherwise it is extraordinary as being one of the very few items of the real Scottish inheritance that have remained more or less intact.

Infinitely more significant in the life of the country, perhaps naturally enough, is the educational system. This has become a legend, to be sure, and a fecund inspiration of sentimentality; and that the system of education in Scotland to-day is superior to that of, say, England is simply not true. (These are not the days of institutional uniqueness!) But still the attitude to education of Scottish teachers, parents and pupils, the methods of education, and the social implications of education affect Scottish life to its very roots.

It started centuries ago with a vast interest and pride in the advantages of learning. John Knox may have got more credit than he deserves for the institution of the parish school, but it certainly was about those humble foundations that a great and noble passion flourished. The poverty of the land was always there to urge the people to effort; the religious obsession moved almost every parent to see a son "wag his heid in the pulpit." Given the deliberate and careful mental habits of the race, Scotland was thus learning long before learning became a matter of compulsion, and long before the typical English peasant could do anything in the way of writing save make his mark or count except with his fingers. It was a passion that, besides producing a race of scholars, had strange and often beautiful social consequences. The crofter family starving so that a talented lad might ultimately go to College in Glasgow; and the lad in turn setting off on foot with a bag of meal for his winter sustenance . . . these are not merely figures of kail-yard romance. They were the real symbols of that vast army of well-informed, capable Scots who, for better or for worse, have given to Empire amazing

114 MAKING THE MOTORIST PAY! The Ferry over Loch Leven at Ballachulish, Argyll

115 FERTILE FARMING COUNTRY ON THE SHORES OF LOCH TAY, PERTHSHIRE

service as pioneers, soldiers, teachers, missionaries and administrators.

The system that grew out of such small beginnings was inevitably democratic. The Public School in the English sense—curiously enough, the term is still used in Scotland of what is officially a state-supported elementary school—could not flourish in the post-Reformation Scotland; and those that have been established during the last century are in purely artificial imitation of a foreign habit, designed in concession to the developing spirit of social self-consciousness.

Virtually the whole of the Scottish educational system is the responsibility of rate- and tax-payer. Few are the institutions that flourish on fees and endowments. Relatively few, indeed, are those run on any sort of fee-paying basis. Scotland has its great Grammar Schools, and hardly one without a splendid record of scholarship. They were at their best the creation mainly of the merchant class—for example, the Grammar School of Aberdeen and the High School of Glasgow—but they were not designed in social intention. They represented the effort to take the education of a boy from a well-to-do home a stage beyond that to which the parish dominie could push only a few choice pupils. In fact, they survive from the days when Scots parents were vastly more willing to pay for the educational advantages of their children than they are now; and if they have nowadays any superiorities over the non-fee-paying Higher Grade schools, such superiorities are merely social.

One is almost tempted into a digression on the ultimate values of State Socialism, but we certainly find in Scotland some astonishing examples of its operations and of how it tends to affect the spirit of a people. In the elementary schools, for instance, the teaching is, perhaps inevitably, in terms of standard English—and it would be interesting to speculate on how far the impact of that standard on native dialect has been responsible for such ugly abortions as, say, the *patois* of Clydeside. We find, creeping through the fabric, like the death-watch beetle, the influences of small snobbery; so that if it is nothing, even desirable, that the Higher Grade school must have its colours and its captain, it is a little bit sad to see the enterprising headmaster of a Grammar School, his innocent eye on the English Public School and the tenets of Oxford, reduce the old free-and-easy organisation of a burghal concern to a nice anglified arrangement of prefects, "houses," and all the apparatus that is familiar to the Scot only through the medium of "school stories."

Now the process goes much further. Your Scot of means will have nothing but Public School education for his sons and daughters. In a certain Scottish town one happens to know well, the departure of a boy for a Public School in England was twenty years ago an event of almost communal interest. Now it is the commonplace among the well-to-do. Higher and higher run the social aspirations. And lower and lower runs the flood of the old national life.

Happily, we are not called upon in this place to pass judgment on the ultimate values of the tendency. Again we simply note the Scottish fate—to lose the aboriginal tradition and to make an uneasy and imperfect adjustment to another that is fundamentally alien. And in the sphere of education the estimation of ultimate values is particularly difficult. For if the Scottish system has the great virtues of thoroughness and utilitarian efficiency, it does not lead naturally to that culture which is the flower of the English system, and which is the product of both educational and social influences working in wellnigh perfect harmony. If the aristocrats and plutocrats of Scotland serve their country ill by insisting on English education for their children, theirs is yet an aspiration to something that Scotland cannot out of its own natural resources provide. Ease and confidence are the last elements to be found in the Scottish make-up.

The break with an old tradition and the failure to work out another to take its place are best exemplified

116 THE PEACE OF SUMMER IN A HIGHLAND GLEN: the Braes o' Balquhidder, Perthshire

117 LOCH NESS, NEAR STROME POINT, ON A CALM DAY

in the cases of the four Scottish Universities. These are of a very respectable antiquity. The oldest, St. Andrews, dates from 1411. Glasgow followed in 1450. Aberdeen was founded in 1494, Edinburgh in 1582. (Strange that the Capital should have been the last to acquire a seat of learning!) These were monkish establishments in the first place, like the colleges of Oxford and Cambridge, and they remained largely residential until about the middle of last century. Then—and the reasons are curious and typical—they suddenly descended to the status of large technical day-schools.

With the growth of wealth during the nineteenth century hundreds of students began to knock at their democratic and inexpensive doors. The industralised condition of the country demanded that many of these students should require purely technical training. The traditional Scots interest in education had endowed them very liberally with bursaries. A degree was always useful to the young Scotsman on the make. So the Universities were overwhelmed by an excess of undergraduates, most of them shaping frankly for a career, whether in the Kirk, medicine or teaching. These lads had to turn to education as the means to the material end. The degree was for bread and butter, a mark of a certain efficiency attained; it ceased to be the laurel of culture acquired. The factory of graduates—and the standard of actual scholarship is not in question at the moment—replaced the seat of lightly worn learning.

That change, in its purely social aspects, has been of immense importance to Scotland. With the passing of the old residential college much that was ultimately valuable was lost. It was the industrial system at its fell work; thenceforward every investment had to have its tangible dividend. The process was perfectly, grimly symbolised in the removal, in 1870, of the University of Glasgow from the lovely seventeenth-century college buildings in the High Street to the present edifice on the crown of Gilmorehill, a typical compromise by Sir

THE MARISCHAL COLLEGE, ABERDEEN

Gilbert Scott between Scots Baronial and Gothic that too often betrays its relationship with St. Pancras Station Hotel. And the retreat of pure scholarship was transformed into a rout when Andrew Carnegie, meaning extremely well, no doubt, set aside a huge sum in trust so that no Scottish boy or girl, being reasonably literate, could fail to enjoy the advantages of a University education.

That finished it. The higher education ceased to be a reward and a dream. It became a reasonable expectation, like the trustworthiness of the municipal electricity supply or the virtual certainty of the arrival of to-morrow morning's post.

Even the layman is entitled to say that a lowering of standards all round was bound to be one result of this process—and sometimes Scotland seems indeed the happy hunting-ground of the imperfectly educated. It is surely manifest that the finest results of collegiate education could not be realised when the residential system collapsed and the undergraduate lost all the benefits of a corporate existence. Wise men realise that now, though they do not often, in Scotland, dare to say it. The most valiant efforts are at this moment being made to restore to St. Andrews and Aberdeen in particular the original intra-mural character. In Glasgow and Edinburgh, with their thousands of students, the difficulties are greater, almost insuperable, but still one sees the effort of authority nowadays to revive the corporate spirit. May it succeed! But will it? For many a day to come, we may agree, the truly able Scot will still have to go to Oxford or Cambridge for his ultimate learning, unless very specially favoured under the native system. And it is worth noting that the Faculties of the four Universities are largely recruited from men who have lingered awhile by Isis or Cam.

And here we have perhaps, at the end of our journey, the handiest possible illustration of the state of Scotland's heart at this moment of writing on a lovely evening of

May 1934. As among all the influences that have impinged upon it—the religious, the industrial and the alien—it is uneasily, rather unhappily and quite uncertainly balanced. If it has a native civilisation, that is only vestigial now. And yet it remains, because of the stubborn fact of nationality, imperfectly absorbed into any other.

The conditions of the arts in Scotland witness powerfully to the confused state of her soul. Putting it at its very roughest, it could be said that the Scottish people have a decided interest in pictorial art, in music and, latterly, in the drama, and none at all worth talking about in literature and architecture. It is perfectly true that Scotland is a rich market for good books, but there is absolutely no discernible bias towards books of purely Scottish character, unless they be of the romantic order. It is a hard thing to say, but it is a fact of publishing that Scotland will not enthusiastically accept a Scottish book until that book has received the imprimatur of London. Left to itself, it will read only such books as present the romantic aspects of the country's history and hymn the glory of scenery. It may be vastly flattered when an alien—an L. A. G. Strong, an H. V. Morton or a Maurice Walsh—selects Albyn for the setting of his travel essays or of a piece of fiction; it will even accept harsh criticism from a foreigner; but it shies away, as from a betrayal, from criticism of Scotland by Scotsmen in contemporary terms and, in reaction, takes, like the clansmen of old, to the heather. And that is tremendously typical and significant.

The relative lack of interest in architecture, in the decencies of building, ought by now to be understandable enough. For that the rebellion of the Reformed Kirk, with considerable help from the industrialists, must take the blame. (And how the repressions of the early Kirk favoured a peculiarly brutal type of industrialism is a subject of inquiry worth a volume in itself.) But a sensitiveness to musical influences, a genuine interest in

118 A PERTHSHIRE PANORAMA, WITH THE RIVER TAY AND BIRNAM WOODS, FAMOUS IN "MACBETH"

119 LOW TIDE AT LITTLE FERRY, GOLSPIE, SUTHERLAND

120 A SETTLEMENT ON THE WESTERN SEABOARD: Easdale, on the Island of Seil, Argyllshire

121 THE LAST OF THE MAINLAND: an Air View of " John o' Groats " shelving into the Northern Seas

painting, and the new-found enthusiasm for community drama do bespeak an intensity of aesthetic interest not frequently credited to the race.

It was in no way remarkable that Edinburgh should have housed a Raeburn rather more than a hundred years ago. Edinburgh was then still a Capital in effect, with its own metropolitan society and its own field for the full deployment and employment of native genius; and all we need observe is that a Raeburn of this fourth decade of the twentieth century would assuredly prefer to operate in London. What was really remarkable was the appearance in Glasgow, of all improbable places, and at the height of the city's industrial prosperity during the last decades of the nineteenth century, of a school of artists who made that grey industrial municipality of the North for a space one of the art capitals of Europe.

The men of the Glasgow School were revolutionaries in their day. As happened in the case of the Law, England was short-circuited and a progressive idea brought straight from France. The Scottish colourists leapt straight into European fame while England was still wallowing in the simple faith that the glossy prints of Alma Tadema represented the limit of pictorial achievement. At or about the same time the great Scottish etchers—Strang, Cameron and Bone—were thrusting forward a new conception of that austere art. It was a truly remarkable period; and if the atmospherics of the Glasgow School are now *vieux jeux*, and the sentimentalities of the popular passion for etchings now exposed, the episode is not to be forgotten in any survey of European art nor the distinctively Scottish contribution underrated.

At the same time, we have to observe some highly characteristic limitations of that remarkable movement. We note, in the first place, that the revolution of the Glasgow School was concerned with the methods rather than with the philosophies of painting. Very few Scots artists have ever been anything but severely representational. The Scottish artist may frequently graduate from landscape to the more profitable pursuit of portraiture, but the facts that landscape is his most natural mode of expression, and that the Scottish public most warmly appreciates renderings of the country's superlative landscape, are again the sure signs of a national inclination and limitation.

It is the old story of escape from the Scottish topicalities into the Scottish past, that racial need to forget Bellshill in the glamour of the countryside the masses dare not call their own. Here, indeed, we at last discover an instance in which the state of the heart of Scotland is conditioned by the fairness of her face. But we make a sad error of misunderstanding if we mistake for a positive verity what is only a typical nostalgia.

It is much the same with music. The more or less successful existence of the Scottish Orchestra testifies to a decent degree of musical culture in the people, but as it is hardly at all an expression of purely Scottish culture, it is of no more importance in this survey than the Hallé Orchestra of Manchester. Scotland has always been willing to sing the stodgier oratorios, but so have Yorkshire and Lancashire and Wales. Much more to the point is the emergence of such a body as the Orpheus Choir of Glasgow, a rather self-consciously democratic body that has nevertheless set for the whole civilised world new standards of vocalisation and interpretation. It represents a magnificent and truly Scottish achievement; but observe again the nature of the material upon which its success has been built. It sings most mellifluously of the past. The note of yearning is its strongest suit. Seal-women, tearful Hebridean mothers, and comic characters long dead are its stock-in-trade. Nostalgia prevails, and the real Scotland of to-day contributes nothing, or is not permitted to contribute anything, to the performance of this distinguished body of exquisite executants.

But when we turn to the astonishing success of the community drama in Scotland and the real Scottish achievement in that field we encounter a phenomenon extremely puzzling and possibly extremely significant.

It is a recent growth, and all the more important on that account. It has flourished like a tropical plant where all the traditional influences were against indulgences in the dramatic form. Suddenly, over the night that has prevailed since the War, a wave of enthusiasm for this form of expression has swollen to sweep the country, seeping into the most unexpected corners, so that the open competition of 1933, taken part in by hundreds of teams, including the best that the relatively sophisticated societies of Edinburgh and Glasgow could produce, was won by a group of simple but intensely purposeful people from the remote and improbable townlet of Brora in Sutherlandshire. The characteristic taint of the kail-yard may have affected the movement to some extent, but that it is the most progressive, the most vital, the most popular and, at the same time, most truly national type of aesthetic endeavour in modern Scotland it is just impossible to deny.

Is Scotland to surprise itself and the world with a burst of distinction in the theatre? Is the metropolitan success of the Glasgow doctor who calls himself "James Bridie," and is yet so delightfully a purely Scottish figure, only an episode of the moment? We cannot tell, and we need not waste time on speculation. All we have to recognise is that, late in the day, when all the purely Scottish causes seemed hopelessly lost, the people abandoned to sentimentality and romantic nostalgia, as blind to the realities of their country as the veriest Cockney, along comes this movement to declare apparently that the young people of Scotland have it in them, consciously or not, to create a native self-contained art.

What are we to make of it? . . . The wise man will perhaps do best to look on it all as a race between the suppressed but still living instinct of the people and the levelling influences that crowd upon them, by way of

London in particular. Scottish Nationalism, in the political sense, is but the last-ditch expression of the will that the country should not lose its cultural identity.

It is a worthy sentiment, but it has to be feared sometimes that the will is not shared by the Scottish people as a whole. The forces often appear to have been too much for them. Largely huddled into drab industrial towns, they find it sufficient satisfaction to delight in the loveliness of the country round about them, blind to the economic ugliness that its empty and deliberately uncultivated condition represents. Notably slaves of jazz and the cinema, they will defend their unique Scottishness in terms of events and grandeurs long past and sadly soiled. For the most part they sit, curiously complacent, amid the ruins of their own civilisation, such as it was. It has not dawned on them yet that they may shortly be squatting amid the ruins of that industrial civilisation which once allowed them to enjoy the best of both worlds.

The temptation is to express it all in political terms. This people once possessed a nationality, and the forces that tend to destroy the national integrity come largely from the dominant power of England; so that some men see in the breaking of the material English tie the spiritual salvation of Scotland. They may be right, and they may be wrong. They may have come into the field just in time—or they may have come too late. Nothing that they can do may have the effect of turning back the Scottish clock. And what happens to Scotland as a separate entity may not matter at all.

So with that we leave the Scots to the Fates, having learned in the course of our journey, it may be hoped, something of their great indigenous worth, something of their troubles and problems, something of the uneasiness that strange circumstance has forced upon them, and something of their abiding interest as a people in their own right.

INDEX

(The numerals in italic type denote the *figure numbers* of illustrations)

A Selected List of BATSFORD BOOKS

relating to

Architecture, Fine and Decorative Art, Interior Decoration, Gardens, Social History, Crafts, Applied Science, Engineering, etc.

Published by B. T. BATSFORD LTD.

Booksellers and Publishers by appointment to H.M. The Queen

15 North Audley Street, London

CONTENTS

NOTE.—This list comprises about 190 books on the subjects shown above from Batsford's main catalogue, in which are listed some 600 odd titles. It is intended to form a representative selection for the use of readers, but those interested in any particular subject should obtain the main catalogue (which will be sent post free on request), which comprises a much wider range of titles under every head. Fully illustrated prospectuses of most books can also be sent on request. Patrons are reminded that Batsford's new premises are at 15 North Audley Street, London, W.1, one minute from Oxford Street, on the main thoroughfare leading to Grosvenor Square, two minutes' walk from either Bond Street or Marble Arch Stations on the Central London Railway, where their immense stock of books, old and new, English and foreign, with prints, pictures, etc., can be inspected at leisure in the large and beautifully-fitted new showrooms. *Telephone Mayfair 6118; Accounts and Production, Mayfair 4337. Cables: Batsfordia, London. Telegrams: Batsford, Audley, London.*

A full index of the books contained in this list arranged alphabetically under the names of authors, is given on page 32.

List F. 50m. 3 34.

THE CATHEDRALS OF ENGLAND

By HARRY BATSFORD and CHARLES FRY. The letterpress consists of a rapid but comprehensive Introduction, followed by a short, clear description of each cathedral, its situation, history, architecture and romance. There are 133 illustrations from new photographs, which form a superb series, far in advance of anything yet produced on the subject. There are also a colour Frontispiece from an old drawing by F. Mackenzie, and some 30 Line Sketches in the text by BRIAN COOK. The book is the ideal guide for the modern tourist, untechnical but absolutely reliable, superbly produced and illustrated. Demy 8vo, cloth, lettered. 7s. 6d. net.

THE ENGLISH VILLAGE

By SIR JOHN SQUIRE. This book is the work not only of a famous man of letters, but of one who has fought unceasingly for the preservation of the English countryside, of which his knowledge is extraordinarily wide and comprehensive. As a treatise on the English Village, its life, character, history and architecture, it will be appreciated by all who love the tranquil charm and fine old craftsmanship of these beautiful survivals. There are 130 superb illustrations from new Photographs and twenty Drawings in the text by SYDNEY R. JONES. Demy 8vo, cloth, lettered. 7s. 6d. net.

THE OLD INNS OF ENGLAND

By A. E. RICHARDSON, F.S.A. This volume constitutes a comprehensive survey of the fine old inns that are one of the most attractive features of the English towns and villages. It is a fascinating subject, embracing the whole life of the roads through England's history, and Professor Richardson has done full justice to it in a letterpress that is full of knowledge and robust humour. It is illustrated by 130 fine new Photographs of inns, medieval and later, in stone or timber, and there are in addition 20 Line Drawings by BRIAN COOK. The book is an indispensable possession to the motorist. Demy 8vo, cloth, lettered. 7s. 6d. net.

THE FACE OF SCOTLAND

A Pictorial Review of its Scenery: Hills, Glens, Lochs, Coast, Islands, Moors, etc., with Old Buildings, Castles, Churches, etc. Including a brief review of Topography, History and Characteristics. By HARRY BATSFORD and CHARLES FRY, with a foreword by JOHN BUCHAN, C.H., M.P. With 130 splendid illustrations, from specially selected Photographs, many hitherto unpublished, a Frontispiece in colour from a Water-colour by W. RUSSELL FLINT, R.A., and numerous Line Drawings in the text by BRIAN COOK. Demy 8vo, cloth, lettered. 7s. 6d. net.

THE "ENGLISH LIFE" SERIES

THE LANDSCAPE OF ENGLAND

By CHARLES BRADLEY FORD. With a Foreword by Professor G. M. TREVELYAN, O.M., M.A., F.S.A., etc. An attractive, popular, yet systematic and informative survey under 5 main divisions: North, Midlands, East, South-East, and West Country. With 135 fine Photographic Illustrations, mostly full-page and largely unpublished, including also a coloured Frontispiece, 25 Pen Drawings and 6 Maps, by BRIAN COOK. Large 8vo, cloth, lettered. 12s. 6d. net.

"The varied beauties of English landscape are reflected with unusual charm in this treasurable volume. It would seem impossible, indeed, to overpraise the quality of the artistry and skill which has gone to the making of this book. The volume as a whole has been well planned; it is a truly remarkable and appealing production."—*Liverpool Daily Post.*

THE "ENGLISH LIFE" SERIES—(continued)

HOMES AND GARDENS OF ENGLAND

By HARRY BATSFORD, Hon. A.R.I.B.A., and CHARLES FRY. With a Foreword by LORD CONWAY of Allington. An attractive, popular, yet informative survey from the Middle Ages to Victorian Times of old Country Houses and their Gardens. Containing 175 Photographic Illustrations, a Frontispiece in colour by SYDNEY R. JONES, and numerous Line Drawings and Engravings in the text. Large 8vo, cloth, lettered. 12s. 6d. net.

"It is difficult to avoid the appearance of adulation in giving any account of this superbly illustrated production, which at 12s. 6d. gives every indication of philanthropy. The accompanying text is a model of grace and brevity, and the work provides not only an excellent grounding, but its possession is certain to be a continued delight."—*The Bookfinder Illustrated.*

THE ENGLISH COUNTRYSIDE

By ERNEST C. PULBROOK. A Review of some of its Aspects, Features, and Attractions. With 126 Illustrations from Photographs, and a Pencil Frontispiece by A. E. NEWCOMBE. New and cheaper impression. Large 8vo, cloth, gilt. 10s. 6d. net.

ENGLISH COUNTRY LIFE AND WORK

An Account of some Past Aspects and Present Features. By ERNEST C. PULBROOK. Containing about 200 pages on Farmers, Old and New—Field-Work—Cottage Folk—The Village Craftsman—Religious Life, etc. With about 200 artistic Illustrations from special Photographs. A New and cheaper reissue. Large 8vo, cloth, gilt. 12s. 6d. net.

"We may congratulate the author on a very readable and well-illustrated book. He has given a fairly detailed description of a large number of occupations of the English country labourer and village dweller. . . . Such industries as thatching and hurdle-making are described at some length, and there are good pages on country trading."—*The Field.*

OLD ENGLISH HOUSEHOLD LIFE

Some Account of Cottage Objects and Country Folk. By GERTRUDE JEKYLL. Consisting of 17 sections on the Fireplace, Candlelight, the Hearth, the Kitchen, Old Furniture, Home Industries, Cottage Buildings, Itinerants, Mills, Churchyards, etc. With 277 Illustrations from Photographs and Old Prints and Drawings. New and cheaper reissue. Large thick 8vo, cloth, gilt. 12s. 6d. net.

THE COTTAGES OF ENGLAND

A Regional Survey from the XVIth to the XVIIIth Century. By BASIL OLIVER, F.R.I.B.A. The local types of every county are thoroughly represented in about 196 Photographic Illustrations, including 16 Plates in Collotype, and the book forms the most thorough collection yet made of these fine survivals of old English life. With a Frontispiece in colour and a Foreword by the Rt. Hon. STANLEY BALDWIN, M.P. Large 8vo, cloth, gilt, with decorative coloured wrapper. 21s. net.

TOURING ENGLAND BY ROAD AND BYWAY

A Popular Illustrated Guide in a new form to the Beauties of Rural England. By SYDNEY R. JONES. Comprising 20 Typical Tours under Five Divisions, with General Introduction and complete Map, Introduction to each District and specially drawn simplified Route Map of each Tour, which is described in detail, with finger-post reference to features, and buildings of interest. Illustrated by 54 Drawings, including a number full page, specially drawn by the Author, and 50 Illustrations from Photographs by the Artist and others. New and cheaper issue. Crown 8vo, cloth. 5s. net.

"This little book is a delightful guide to the English countryside, useful alike to walker, cyclist, and motorist."—*Queen.*

LITTLE KNOWN ENGLAND: RAMBLES IN THE WELSH BORDERLAND, THE ROLLING UPLANDS, THE CHALK HILLS, AND THE EASTERN COUNTIES

By HAROLD DONALDSON EBERLEIN, Author of numerous works on Architecture, Decoration and Furniture. With about 120 Illustrations, 80 from Photographs and Paintings, and 40 in the text from Drawings, Sketches, Engravings, etc. Including a series of Maps. 8vo, cloth, lettered. 12s. 6d. net.

GEORGIAN ENGLAND (1700-1830)

A Review of its Social Life, Arts and Industries. By Professor A. E. RICHARDSON, F.S.A., F.R.I.B.A., Author of "The English Inn," etc. Containing sections on the Social Scene, Navy, Army, Church, Sport, Architecture, Building Crafts, the Trades, Decorative Arts, Painting, Literature, Theatres, etc. Illustrated by 200 subjects from Photographs and contemporary Prints, Engravings and Drawings, by Hogarth, Wheatley, Gainsborough, Reynolds, Rowlandson, and other artists. With 54 Line Text Illustrations, largely unpublished, and a Colour Frontispiece from an unpublished aquatint by ROBERT DIGHTON. Med. 8vo, cloth, gilt. 21s. net.

A TOUR THRO' LONDON ABOUT THE YEAR 1725

Being Letter V and parts of Letter VI of "A Tour Thro' the Whole Island of Great Britain." Containing a description of the City of London, taking in the City of Westminster, Borough of Southwark and Parts of Middlesex. By DANIEL DEFOE. Reprinted from the Original Edition (1724-1726). Edited and Annotated by SIR MAYSON BEETON, K.B.E., M.A., and E. BERESFORD CHANCELLOR, M.A., F.S.A. With Introduction, Prefatory Note, etc. Illustrated by 2 contemporary (end paper) and 4 specially drawn folding Maps and 56 full-page Plates, 16 hand-printed in Photogravure and the rest in Collotype, representing some 80 Buildings (many now vanished), Squares, Markets, Assemblies, the River, etc., from contemporary Prints, etc. Small folio, antique panelled, calf, gilt, gilt top. £11 11s. net; or in cloth, gilt, antique style, £8 8s. net.

Edition limited to 350 copies, of which but few remain for sale.

TOURING LONDON

By W. TEIGNMOUTH SHORE, Author of "Dinner Building," etc. With an Introduction by the Rt. Hon. JOHN BURNS, P.C. A Series of 4 Tours covering the chief parts of Inner London, written in a bright and pleasant style, but conveying much practical and historical information. Illustrated by 28 Photographs, with Drawings and Sketches in the text by well-known artists. Also a two-colour Map of the city, and Plans. Cheaper reissue. Large crown 8vo, cloth. 2s. 6d. net.

HISTORIC COSTUME

A Chronicle of Fashion in Western Europe, 1490-1790. By FRANCIS M. KELLY and RANDOLPH SCHWABE. Containing the chief characteristics of Dress in each century. Illustrated by some hundreds of full-page and text Sketches from original sources by RANDOLPH SCHWABE of typical groups, figures and details. Including 7 Plates specially reproduced in colour, and 70 Photographic reproductions of Historic Pictures, Portraits, Scenes, etc. Second Edition revised and enlarged. Large Royal 8vo, cloth, gilt, 25s. net.

"Intended primarily for the costumier, film producer, and artist, it is full of delight for the ordinary reader, who will find it an excellent help in the pleasant game of trying to construct a livelier vision of the past."—*The Queen.*

A SHORT HISTORY OF COSTUME AND ARMOUR, CHIEFLY IN ENGLAND, 1066-1800

By F. M. Kelly and Randolph Schwabe, Principal of the Slade School of Fine Art. Royal 8vo, cloth, gilt. 25s. net. Or in 2 volumes:

I. THE MIDDLE AGES, 1066-1485. With Sections on Civilian Dress: "Shirts," "Shapes," Houppelandes and Burgundian Modes; Armour. Illustrated by 4 Plates in colours and gold, over 100 special Pen Drawings by Randolph Schwabe from original sources and 32 Photographic Plates of over 70 reproductions. Royal 8vo, cloth, gilt. 13s. net.

II. THE RENAISSANCE, 1485-1800. With Sections on Puff and Slashes, The Spanish Trend, "Cavalier" and French Modes, the Heyday and Decline of Powder, Armour, etc. Illustrated by 5 Plates (3 double) in colours and gold, over 100 special Pen Drawings by Randolph Schwabe from original sources, 36 Photographic Plates of 58 Reproductions. Royal 8vo, cloth, gilt. 13s. net.

"Within its limits, it is undoubtedly the best book of its kind. Like their previous work, this present history is remarkable at once for its compression and its detail. The number of the illustrations alone is impressive, even more so is their quality. They make a picture-gallery of the past that will delight the ordinary reader almost as much as it will profit the student."—*Times Literary Supplement.*

MEDIAEVAL COSTUME AND LIFE

An Historic and Practical Review. By Dorothy Hartley. Containing 22 full-page Plates from Photographs of living Male and Female Figures in specially made Costumes from Mediaeval MSS., 20 Plates in Line from the Author's Drawings of practical Construction, Detail, Sketches, etc., and 40 Plates of some 200 Reproductions from Contemporary Manuscripts of scenes of Mediæval life and work. Including full historical and descriptive text, with directions for the practical cutting out and making of many costumes illustrated. Large royal 8vo, cloth. 12s. net.

"Miss Hartley has treated the subject in a refreshingly original manner. She gives a great deal of practical advice, and the whole pageant of costume is linked up with society in such a way that we get a startlingly definite view of daily life and work. Altogether a fascinating handbook."—*Sunday Times.*

THE "PEOPLE'S LIFE AND WORK" SERIES

LIFE AND WORK OF THE ENGLISH PEOPLE THROUGH THE CENTURIES

A Pictorial Record from Contemporary Sources. By Dorothy Hartley and Margaret M. Elliot, B.A. (Lond.). Each volume is devoted to a separate century and contains 32 pp. of Text and about 150 pictures on 48 full-page Plates of Household Life, Crafts and Industries, Building, Farming, Warfare, City and Country Scenes, Transport, Children, Church Life, Gardens, etc. With an Introduction on the characteristics of each period, full Descriptive Notes, Historical Chart, Analytical Index, Music, etc. Large (royal) 8vo, boards, lettered, or in portfolio with flaps 3s. net per volume; or in cloth, 3s. 6d. net per volume. Volumes I and II (Early Middle Ages), III and IV (Later Middle Ages), and V and VI (Renaissance) are also bound together in cloth, 6s. net each, and volumes I, II and III (Middle Ages), and IV, V and VI (Renaissance) are also combined in cloth at 9s. net each. A few remaining copies of volumes II and III (Later Middle Ages), and volumes IV and V (Early and Middle Renaissance), can also be obtained bound together in cloth at 5s. net each.

The Series has now been completed as follows:

I. SAXON TIMES TO 1300
II. THE FOURTEENTH CENTURY
III. THE FIFTEENTH CENTURY
IV. THE SIXTEENTH CENTURY
V. THE SEVENTEENTH CENTURY
VI. THE EIGHTEENTH CENTURY

"A delightful collection of contemporary pictures largely taken from manuscripts. Of recent years we have had a bewildering output of picture-books, but we do not know of any on such a scale as this, cheap enough to find their way into the actual possession of children."—*The Manchester Guardian.*

The Quennell Series of Books on Social Life and History

"In their volumes the authors have covered history from the Old Stone Age to the Industrial Revolution. They have approached history from a new angle and in the process have revolutionised the teaching of it. In their hands it has become a live, vivid, and picturesque subject, for they have breathed new life into old bones. Their methods in narrative and illustration are now widely and generally recognised and appreciated." *Western Mail.*

A HISTORY OF EVERYDAY THINGS IN ENGLAND, 1066-1799

Written and Illustrated by MARJORIE and C. H. B. QUENNELL. In Two Volumes. Medium 8vo. 8s. 6d. net each; also issued bound in one volume, 16s. 6d. net.

This account of the English People in their everyday life, of their occupations and amusements during seven centuries, may be read with enjoyment by all interested in the life of Great Britain. The book appeals strongly to Students, Designers, and those interested in Buildings, Decoration, and Costume.

VOL. I.—EVERYDAY THINGS IN ENGLAND, 1066-1499

With 90 Illustrations, many full-page, and 3 Plates in colour. Second Edition, revised and enlarged, with additional illustrations.

VOL. II.—EVERYDAY THINGS IN ENGLAND, 1500-1799

By MARJORIE and C. H. B. QUENNELL. With 4 Coloured Plates and 111 other Illustrations from the Author's Drawings. Second Edition, revised and enlarged, with additional Illustrations.

Issued in Parts for Schools and Class Teaching

The work is now obtainable in Six Separate Parts, each covering a period of history of about a century, appropriate for a term's study. Each part has its own TITLE, CONTENTS, and FULL INDEX; the ILLUSTRATIONS are all given, and the coloured plates and comparative charts are also included. Bound in stiff paper covers (with the original special design), at 3s. net each part.

PART I. ENGLAND UNDER FOREIGN KINGS (1066-1199). Containing 2 Colour Plates, 5 full-page line Illustrations, and 15 in the text.

PART II. THE RISE OF PARLIAMENT (1200-1399). Containing 2 Colour Plates, 8 full-page Illustrations, and 22 in the text.

PART III. THE HUNDRED YEARS' WAR (1400-1499). Containing 1 Colour Plate, 11 full-page line Illustrations, and 13 in the text.

PART IV. THE AGE OF ADVENTURE (1500-1599). Containing 2 Colour Plates, 16 full-page line Illustrations, and 30 in the text.

PART V. THE CROWN'S BID FOR POWER (1600-1699). Containing 1 Colour Plate, 11 full-page line Illustrations, and 21 in the text.

PART VI. THE RISE OF MODERN ENGLAND (1700-1799). Containing 1 Colour Plate, 11 full-page line Illustrations, and 19 in the text.

VOL. III.—EVERYDAY THINGS IN ENGLAND, 1733-1851

THE COMING OF THE INDUSTRIAL ERA. An Account of the Transition from Traditional to Modern Life and Civilization. Written and Illustrated by MARJORIE and C. H. B. QUENNELL. Tracing the Transformation of Agriculture, the coming of Steam Power, the application of Inventions, Trends in Social Life in Town and Country, Costume, Building, etc. Illustrated by 4 Coloured Plates, 120 full-page and smaller Drawings specially prepared by the Authors, and a series of Reproductions of contemporary Engravings and Drawings. Medium 8vo, art canvas. 8s. 6d. net.

THE EVERYDAY LIFE SERIES

A Graphic and Popular Survey of the Efforts and Progress of the Human Race, now completed in 4 volumes. Crown 8vo. cloth. 5s. net. each.

EVERYDAY LIFE IN THE OLD STONE AGE

Written and Illustrated by MARJORIE and C. H. B. QUENNELL. Containing 128 pages, including 70 Illustrations, and a coloured Frontispiece, from the Authors' Drawings, with a Chronological Chart. Second Edition, revised.

"A small book containing much substance. . . . A vivid, simple style and sprightly humour—which last is carried even into their clever black-and-white illustrations—should give them many appreciative readers. A most attractive little book."—*The Morning Post.*

EVERYDAY LIFE IN THE NEW STONE, BRONZE AND EARLY IRON AGES

Written and Illustrated by MARJORIE and C. H. B. QUENNELL. Containing 144 pages, with 90 original Illustrations from the Authors' Drawings, of Household Life, Agriculture, Pottery, Weapons, Ornaments, etc., including 2 Plates in colour, a marked Map, and a Chronological Chart. Second Edition, revised.

The above two works may now be obtained bound in one handy volume as described below:

EVERYDAY LIFE IN PREHISTORIC TIMES

Containing 272 pages, 3 Plates in colour and 2 in monochrome, with 160 Illustrations from the Authors' Pen-and-Ink Drawings, two Chronological Charts and a Comparative Map. The Old Stone Age Section has an Account of the Rhodesian Skull and Nebraskan Tooth, with 2 additional Illustrations. Crown 8vo, cloth, lettered. 10s. net.

EVERYDAY LIFE IN ROMAN BRITAIN

Written and Illustrated by MARJORIE and C. H. B. QUENNELL. Containing 128 pages, with over 100 original Illustrations from the Authors' Pen Drawings, of Cities and Camps, Villas, Ships, Chariots, Monuments, Costume, Military Life, Household Objects, Pottery, etc. Including 3 Colour Plates, Chart, and Map of Roads.

EVERYDAY LIFE IN SAXON, VIKING, AND NORMAN TIMES

Written and Illustrated by MARJORIE and C. H. B. QUENNELL. Containing 128 pages, with over 100 original Illustrations from the Authors' Pen and Pencil Drawings of Ships, Cooking, Metalwork, Caskets, Crosses, Buildings, Pottery, and Illuminated MSS., including 2 coloured Plates, Historical Chart, etc. Crown 8vo, cloth. 5s. net.

"It is a period which gives scope for interesting writing and delightful illustrations. The authors have, as before, profited to the full by their opportunities. Altogether this is an agreeable as well as a valuable book, and one can say of the authors what Asser said of Alfred. They are 'affable and pleasant to all, and curiously eager to vestigate things unknown.' "—*The Times.*

ENGLAND IN TUDOR TIMES

An Account of its Social Life and Industries. By L. F. SALZMAN, M.A., F.S.A., Author of "English Industries of the Middle Ages," etc. A remarkable survey of a great period in England's Social history. Containing chapters on The Spirit of the Tudor Age—Life in the Country—Life in the Town—Life in the Home—The Church—Adventure on Land and Sea. With 138 pages of text, 64 full-page illustrations and plentiful illustrations in the text from Drawings, Engravings, etc. Cheaper reissue. Demy 8vo., cloth. 5s. net.

A New Fascinating Series of Classical Social Life. Uniform with the Author's "Everyday Things in England."

EVERYDAY THINGS IN ANCIENT GREECE (HOMERIC—ARCHAIC—CLASSICAL)

An "Omnibus" Volume of the three following works. Written and Illustrated by MARJORIE and C. H. B. QUENNELL. A full review of Social Life and the Arts. Containing 3 coloured Plates, some 238 full-page and smaller Illustrations from Drawings in Pen-and-Ink, Pencil, and Wash and 20 from Photographs. Large thick 8vo. 21s. net.

VOL. I. EVERYDAY THINGS IN HOMERIC GREECE

Written and Illustrated by MARJORIE and C. H. B. QUENNELL, Authors of "The Everyday Life Series," etc. Presenting a vivid picture based on the Social Life in the Iliad and Odyssey, etc. Illustrated by about 70 full-page and smaller Drawings by the Authors, after early Vase Paintings and their own restorations. With Colour Frontispiece, Photographic Illustrations, Map, etc. Large 8vo, decoratively bound. 7s. 6d. net.

VOL. II. EVERYDAY THINGS IN ARCHAIC GREECE

Written and Illustrated by MARJORIE and C. H. B. QUENNELL. A Graphic Account of Social Life from the close of the Trojan War to the Persian Struggle, treating of Herodotus and his History, the Temple and the House, Life inside the House, and Life outside the House. Illustrated by 85 full-page and smaller Drawings by the Authors, specially prepared for the book· With a coloured Frontispiece, a number of Photographic Illustrations, Map, etc. Large 8vo, cloth, lettered. 7s. 6d. net.

"The Quennell books are likely to outlast some of the most imposing institutions of the post-war world. A book which is written with great scholarship and surprising lucidity. To speak in superlatives of this series is only justice, for seldom is there found such a unity between publisher, author, and illustrator as the Batsford books display."—*G. K.'s Weekly.*

VOL. III. EVERYDAY THINGS IN CLASSICAL GREECE

Written and Illustrated by MARJORIE and C. H. B. QUENNELL. A vivid picture of Social Life in the Golden Age of Pericles, Socrates, Phidias, Plato, and the building of the Parthenon, 480-404 B.C. With Sections on Architecture; The Town and its Planning; Town Houses and Everuday Life; Sea Fights and Land Battles, etc. Illustrated by 83 full-page and smaller Pen-and-Ink or Wash Drawings specially made by the Authors. With coloured Frontispiece, Series of Photographic Illustrations, Historical Chart, Map, etc. Large 8vo, cloth, lettered. 8s. net.

If ordered at one time the three volumes of this series are priced at 22s. net.

"ESSENTIALS OF LIFE" SERIES

By Lieut.-Colonel F. S. BRERETON, C.B.E. Bright, informative reviews of the Indispensable Things of Human Life. Each with 80 pages of text, and about 100 Illustrations in Line and Half-tone from Photographs, Drawings, Old Prints, etc., of Old and Modern Developments. Large crown 8vo, cloth, lettered. 4s. net each.

I. CLOTHING: An Account of its Types and Manufacture. Contents: Materials—Spinning—Weaving—The Sewing Machine—A Modern Factory—Furs and Rubber—Leather and Tanning—Boots—Hats—Glove-making—Dyeing and Cleaning—Pins—Needles—Buttons, etc.

II. TRAVEL: An Account of its Methods in Past and Present. Contents: Early Roads and Trading Routes—Coaching—The Steam Engine—Steamships and Railways—The Bicycle—The Petrol Engine—Air Travel—Postman—Wire or Wireless. With Illustrations of Coaches, Engines, Balloons, Aircraft, Ships, Steamers, etc.

"Each volume is illustrated with a wealth of pictures from old and modern sources. The text is written in an easy, discursive style that should popularise the books, and is yet packed with sound knowledge and fact."—*L'Atlantique.*

A HISTORY OF ARCHITECTURE ON THE COMPARATIVE METHOD

For the Student, Craftsman, and Amateur. By Sir BANISTER FLETCHER, PP.R.I.B.A. Eighth Edition, completely re-written. Containing nearly 1000 pages, with about 3500 Illustrations (1560 recently added and nearly 2000 reproduced larger for this Edition), from Photographs and Drawings of Buildings of all Countries and Times. Royal 8vo, cloth, gilt. £2 2s. net.

A SHORT CRITICAL HISTORY OF ARCHITECTURE

By H. HEATHCOTE STATHAM, F.R.I.B.A. Second Edition, revised and enlarged by G. MAXWELL AYLWIN, F.R.I.B.A. Containing 600 pages and 750 Illustrations from Photographs, Drawings, Plans, Prints, etc., with Chronological Charts and Glossary. Demy 8vo, cloth, gilt. 16s. net.

Also supplied in 3 parts, cloth, gilt. 6s. net each.

I. ARCHITECTURE OF ANTIQUITY AND THE CLASSIC AGES.

II. BYZANTINE, ROMANESQUE AND SARACENIC STYLES.

III. THE MIDDLE AGES AND THE RENAISSANCE TO MODERN TIMES.

Eact part contains about 200 pages, with 250 full-page and smaller Illustrations, and is complete with Prefaces, Charts, Glossary and Indexes.

"Within the limits of its size and price it is the most valuable handbook that has appeared in English for those who wish to understand the architecture of the past." —*The Architect.*

THE STORY OF ARCHITECTURE

From the Earliest Ages to the Present Day. By P. LESLIE WATERHOUSE, F.R.I.B.A. With Illustrations of the great buildings of all time from Photographs and Drawings, and many Diagrams in the text. F'Cap 8vo, boards, lettered. 6s. net.

THE STORY OF ARCHITECTURE IN ENGLAND

By WALTER H. GODFREY, F.S.A., F.R.I.B.A. A popular illustrated account, in which the aims and methods of Architectural Design are simply explained, and linked up with the social life of the time. In Two Parts: I. Early and Mediæval, to 1500, chiefly Churches; II. Renaissance, 1500-1800, chiefly Houses. Demy 8vo, cloth. 6s. 6d. net per part; or the two volumes bound in one, 12s. 6d. net.

I. PRE-REFORMATION, THE PERIOD OF CHURCH BUILDING
Illustrated by 133 full-page and smaller Photographs and Drawings. Large crown 8vo, cloth. 6s. 6d. net.

II. RENAISSANCE, THE PERIOD OF HOUSE BUILDING
Illustrated by 150 full-page and smaller photographs and drawings. Large crown 8vo, cloth, 6s. 6d. net.

NEW EDITION REVISED AND ENLARGED NOW READY OF THIS GREAT STANDARD WORK

THE DOMESTIC ARCHITECTURE OF ENGLAND DURING THE TUDOR PERIOD

Illustrated in a Series of Photographs and Measured Drawings of Country Houses, Manor Houses and Other Buildings. By THOMAS GARNER and ARTHUR STRATTON, F.R.I.B.A. Second Edition, Revised and Enlarged, comprising 210 Plates, mostly full page, finely reproduced in Collotype, and 250 pages of Historical and Descriptive Text, including 462 illustrations of Additional Views, Plans, Details, etc., from photographs and drawings, making a total of over 800 Illustrations in all. In two volumes, small folio, buckram, gilt. £9 9s. net the set. (The volumes cannot be obtained separately.)

BATSFORD'S
"HISTORICAL ARCHITECTURAL LIBRARY"
of Standard Textbooks on Classic and Renaissance Architecture.

BYZANTINE ARCHITECTURE AND DECORATION

By J. Arnott Hamilton, M.A., author of "The Churches of Palermo," etc. A careful, scholarly and thorough account of the development and character of constructional methods and decoration, and types of extant buildings in Constantinople, Greece, the Balkans, Cyprus, Armenia, Italy, etc. With 120 Photographic Illustrations of exteriors and interiors, Reconstructions, Constructional Diagrams, Carving, Details, etc., and numerous Line Plans, Measured Drawings, and Sketches in the text. Medium 8vo, cloth, gilt. 18s. net.

ANDERSON AND SPIERS' "ARCHITECTURE OF GREECE AND ROME"

Now reissued in two volumes, obtainable separately, revised and much enlarged. Small Royal 8vo, cloth, gilt. 21s. net each volume, or £2 the two.

I. ARCHITECTURE OF ANCIENT GREECE. Re-written, Remodelled and much enlarged by William Bell Dinsmoor, Professor of Architecture at Columbia University, New York, and the American Academy at Athens. With over 200 Illustrations in Collotype, half-tone and line.

II. ARCHITECTURE OF ANCIENT ROME. Revised and Re-written by Thomas Ashby, Late Director of the British School at Rome. With about 200 Illustrations in half-tone and line.

ARCHITECTURE OF THE RENAISSANCE IN ITALY

By William J. Anderson, A.R.I.B.A. Revised and Enlarged, with an additional Chapter on Baroque and Later work, by Arthur Stratton, F.S.A., F.R.I.B.A. With 80 Plates, including 16 in Collotype, and 120 Illustrations in the text. Small Royal 8vo, cloth, gilt. 21s. net.

ARCHITECTURE OF THE RENAISSANCE IN FRANCE

By W. H. Ward, M.A., F.R.I.B.A. Revised and Enlarged by Sir John W. Simpson, K.B.E., P.P.R.I.B.A. In two volumes, obtainable separately. Small Royal 8vo, cloth, gilt. 21s. net, each volume, or £2 for the two.

IV. THE EARLY RENAISSANCE (1495-1640). With 259 Illustrations.

V. THE LATER RENAISSANCE (1640-1830). With 214 Illustrations.

RENAISSANCE PALACES OF NORTHERN ITALY

(With some Buildings of Earlier Periods). A General Review from the XIIIth to the XVIIth Centuries. Revised and Edited by Professor Dr. Albrecht Haupt. A Condensed Edition in 3 vols. of this Great Standard Work, each containing 160 full-page Plates, reproduced in Collotype from specially taken Photographs or from Measured Drawings expressly prepared. With full historical and descriptive text. Vol. I., TUSCANY, Florence, Pisa, Siena, Montepulciano, Lucca, Pistoia, etc.; Vol. II., VENICE, including also Verona, Mantua, Vicenza, and Padua; Vol. III., GENOA, including also Bologna, Ferrara, Modena, Milan, Turin, Pavia, Bergamo, Brescia, etc. Small folio, cloth, lettered, £2 15s. net each volume, or the set of 3 for £7 10s. net.

"One of the most welcome publications which has issued from the House of Batsford. Their convenient size and excellent quality will appeal to those who are probably deterred by the cost and large size of many fine architectural works. They will be a source of continued delight and interest."—*The Builder*.

A NEW AND IMPORTANT SERIES OF SCHOOL WALL CHARTS

In Two Series now ready, consisting of 25 large lithographed Plates, 30 in. by 20 in. Price Complete 25s. net on stout paper; or £3 2s. od. net mounted on linen, with bound edges. Single diagrams, 1s. 4d. net each; or mounted, 2s. 10d. net each. Introductory Handbook to each Series, 1s. 6d. net each, stiff paper covers, 2s. 6d. net each, cloth, lettered.

THE STYLES OF ENGLISH ARCHITECTURE

A SERIES OF COMPARATIVE WALL OR LECTURE DIAGRAMS. For Schools, Teachers, Students, etc. By ARTHUR STRATTON, F.S.A., F.R.I.B.A. Series I.: THE MIDDLE AGES (Saxon Times to the Start of the Tudor Period). Consisting of 13 large double crown Plates, 20 in. by 30 in. clearly lithographed from the Author's specially prepared Drawings. 13s. net paper, 32s. net mounted.

Series II: THE RENAISSANCE (Tudor, Elizabethan, Stuart, and Georgian Periods). Comprising 12 large diagrams, as in Series I. 12s. net paper, 30s. net mounted.

The 32 pp. Introductory Handbooks contain reduced reproductions of all the Plates with all their sources noted, and an outline account of each style with numerous further Line Illustrations in the text.

ELEMENTS OF FORM AND DESIGN IN CLASSIC ARCHITECTURE

Shown in Exterior and Interior Motives collated from Fine Buildings of all Times. By ARTHUR STRATTON, F.S.A., F.R.I.B.A. Presenting in 80 full-page Plates about 600 motives of Façades, Loggias, Halls, Staircases, etc. Including a Series of 16 Plates of Classic and Renaissance Compositions and Designs. With Introduction, Analytical Account to each Section. Descriptive Notes, and Foreword by Prof. A. E. RICHARDSON, F.S.A., F.R.I.B.A. 4to, cloth, gilt. 28s. net.

THE ORDERS OF ARCHITECTURE

GREEK, ROMAN, and RENAISSANCE; with EXAMPLES of their historic APPLICATION IN ITALIAN, FRENCH, ENGLISH, and AMERICAN COLONIAL. By ARTHUR STRATTON, F.S.A. With an Introduction by A. TRYSTAN EDWARDS, A.R.I.B.A. Illustrated in a Series of 80 full-page Plates from Drawings, mostly specially prepared, including a complete series of Vignola's Orders, and rendered examples of French, Italian, and English buildings. With full historical and practical notes and numerous Text Illustrations. 4to, cloth, gilt, or in portfolio, 21s. net; or in 3 parts: CLASSIC, ITALIAN, and APPLICATIONS, cloth 8s. net each.

THE ORDERS OF ARCHITECTURE

By R. PHENÉ SPIERS, F.S.A., F.R.I.B.A. A collection of typical Examples of the Greek, Roman and Italian Orders selected from Normand's "Parallels" and other Authorities, with Notes on Origin and Development and descriptions of the Plates, Revised Bibliography, etc. Fifth Edition, revised and enlarged, containing 27 full-page Plates. Large 4to, half-cloth. 12s. 6d. net.

"An indispensable possession to all students of architecture."—*The Architect.*

ANCIENT ARCHITECTURE, PREHISTORIC, EGYPTIAN, WEST ASIAN, GREEK & ROMAN

A Chronicle in Verse, by H. CHESTER JONES, M.A., F.S.A. Comprising also an outline history of Architecture, brief Prose Introductions to each Section, and a full Glossary of Terms, etc. Illustrated by numerous large Charts and Compositions and many Drawings and Plans of Buildings by the Author. Including a photogravure portrait and appreciative Forewords by Sir EDWIN LUTYENS, R.A., Dr. HADEN GUEST, M.P., and others. Large 8vo, cloth, gilt. 15s. net.

THE GROWTH OF THE ENGLISH HOUSE

A short History of its Design and Development from 1100 to 1800 A.D. By J. ALFRED GOTCH, F.S.A., PP.R.I.B.A. Containing 300 pages, with over 150 Illustrations from Photographs, and many pictures in the text from Measured Drawings, Sketches, Plans, and Old Prints. Second Edition, revised and enlarged. Large crown 8vo, cloth, gilt. 12s. 6d. net.

THE SMALLER ENGLISH HOUSE FROM THE RESTORATION TO THE VICTORIAN ERA, 1660-1840

By A. E. RICHARDSON, F.S.A., F.R.I.B.A., and HAROLD DONALDSON EBERLEIN, B.A. Treating of the Characteristics and Periods of Style; the Evolution of Plan; Materials and Craftsmanship: Roofing, Windows, Ironwork, Fireplaces, Staircases, Wall Treatment, Ceilings. With over 200 Illustrations, many full page, from Photographs and Drawings. Demy 4to, cloth, gilt. Cheaper reissue, 15s. net.

ENGLISH GOTHIC CHURCHES

THE STORY OF THEIR ARCHITECTURE. By CHARLES W. BUDDEN, M.A. A simple, informative account of the Planning, Design, and Details of Parish Churches, Cathedrals, etc., 1066-1500, including Chapters on Local Building, Towers, Spires, Ornaments, etc. Illustrated by 53 Plans and Line Diagrams, and 40 Photographic Plates of 80 Views and Details, including a County List of the chief Churches worth seeing. Crown 8vo, cloth, cheaper reissue, 5s. net.

THE "COUNTY CHURCH" SERIES

Edited by the Rev. J. C. Cox, LL.D., F.S.A. Twelve volumes, each containing numerous Plates from Photographs, and Illustrations from Drawings in the text. F'Cap 8vo, cloth, gilt. 2s. 6d. net per volume.

- CAMBRIDGESHIRE AND THE ISLE OF ELY. By C. H. EVELYN-WHITE, F.S.A.
- CORNWALL. By J. C. Cox, LL.D., F.S.A.
- CUMBERLAND AND WESTMORLAND. By J. C. Cox, LL.D., F.S.A.
- ISLE OF WIGHT. By J. C. Cox, LL.D., F.S.A.
- KENT (2 Vols. sold separately). By F. GRAYLING.
- NORFOLK (2 Vols.). Second Edition, revised and extended. By J. C. Cox, LL.D., F.S.A. (*Now out of print.*)
- NOTTINGHAMSHIRE. By J. C. Cox, LL.D., F.S.A.
- SURREY. By J. E. MORRIS, B.A.
- SUFFOLK (2 Vols. sold separately). By T. H. BRYANT.

OLD CROSSES AND LYCHGATES

A Study of their Design and Craftsmanship. By AYMER VALLANCE, M.A., F.S.A. With over 200 fine Illustrations from specially taken Photographs, Old Prints, and Drawings. Crown 4to, art linen. Cheaper reissue 12s. 6d. net.

ENGLISH CHURCH WOODWORK AND FURNITURE

A Study in Craftsmanship from A.D. 1250-1550. By F. E. HOWARD and F. H. CROSSLEY, F.S.A. Illustrating, in over 480 examples from Photographs, the Development of Screens, Stalls, Benches, Font-Covers, Roofs, Doors, Porches, etc., with details of the Carved and Painted Decoration, etc., etc. Second and cheaper Edition, revised, with a new series of 16 Collotype Plates. Crown 4to, cloth, gilt. 25s. net.

"As a treasury of examples, a large proportion of them almost unknown, and as a compendium of information and research, it is a possession of special interest and value. . . ."—*The Times Literary Supplement.*

ENGLISH CHURCH FITTINGS AND FURNITURE

By the Rev. J. C. Cox, LL.D., F.S.A. A Popular Survey, treating of Churchyards, Bells, Fonts and Covers, Pulpits, Lecterns, Screens, Chained Books, Stained Glass, Organs, Plate and other features of interest. With upwards of 250 Illustrations from Photographs and Drawings. 8vo, cloth, gilt. New and cheaper reissue. 12s. 6d. net.

ENGLISH CHURCH MONUMENTS, A.D. 1150-1550

By F. H. Crossley, F.S.A. A survey of the work of the old English craftsmen in stone, marble, and alabaster. Containing over 250 pages, with upwards of 350 Illustrations, from special Photographs and Drawings. Crown 4to, cloth, gilt. Cheaper reissue 21s. net.

ENGLISH MURAL MONUMENTS AND TOMBSTONES

A Collection of Eighty-four Full-page Photographic Plates of Wall Tablets, Table Tombs, and Headstones of the Seventeenth and Eighteenth Centuries, specially selected by Herbert Batsford for the use of Craftsmen. With an Introduction by W. H. Godfrey, F.S.A. Crown 4to, cloth, gilt. 15s. net.

ANCIENT CHURCH CHESTS AND CHAIRS IN THE HOME COUNTIES ROUND GREATER LONDON

With some Reference to their Surroundings. By Fred Roe, R.I., R.B.C. With a Foreword by C. Reginald Grundy. A survey of the finest of these survivals of ancient craftsmanship by the leading authority on the subject. With 95 Illustrations, many full page, from Drawings by the Author and from Photographs, and a number of Line Illustrations in the text. Cheaper reissue. Demy 4to, cloth, gilt. 12s. 6d. net.

EARLY CHURCH ART IN NORTHERN EUROPE

With special Reference to Timber Construction and Decoration. By Josef Strzygowski, Author of "Origin of Christian Church Art," etc. Dealing with Pre-Romanesque Art of the Croatians; Wooden Architecture in Eastern Europe; Half-Timber Churches in Western Europe; The Mast Churches of Norway; Royal Tombs in Scandinavia. With 190 Illustrations. Royal 8vo, cloth, gilt. 21s. net.

"Present-day writers on architecture cannot be said to be exactly exciting; but Prof. Strzygowski is the exception. For vigour and vehemence he is unsurpassed. A remarkable book, with very much to study in it, if not always to convince."—The Dean of Winchester in *The Sunday Times*.

ENGLISH RENAISSANCE WOODWORK, 1660-1730

A Selection of the finest examples, monumental and domestic, chiefly of the Period of Sir Christopher Wren. By Thomas J. Beveridge. A Series of 80 fine Plates from the Author's measured drawings, specially prepared and fully detailed, including Monographs on St. Paul's Choir Stalls, Hampton Court, Oxford and Cambridge Colleges, London City Churches, etc. Including a series of Collotype Plates from pencil drawings, and illustrated descriptive text. Large folio, half-bound, £3 net (originally published at £6 6s. net).

ENGLISH LEADWORK: ITS ART AND HISTORY

A Book for Architects, Antiquaries, Craftsmen, and Owners and Lovers of Gardens. By Sir Lawrence Weaver, F.S.A. Containing 280 pages, with 441 Illustrations from Photographs and Drawings. Large 4to, art linen, gilt. 30s. net.

ENGLISH INTERIORS FROM SMALLER HOUSES OF THE XVIIth TO XIXth CENTURIES, 1660-1820

By M. JOURDAIN. Illustrating the simpler type of Design during the Stuart, Georgian, and Regency Periods. Containing 200 pages, and 100 Plates, comprising 200 Illustrations, from Photographs and Measured Drawings of Interiors, Chimney-pieces, Staircases, Doors, Ceilings, Panelling, Metalwork, Carving, etc., from minor Country and Town Houses. With Introduction and Historical Notes. Cheaper reissue. Large 4to, cloth, gilt. 15s. net.

OLD ENGLISH FURNITURE FOR THE SMALL COLLECTOR

Its History, Types and Surroundings from Mediæval to Early Victorian Times. By J. P. BLAKE and A. E. REVEIRS-HOPKINS. Containing 150 pages with about 130 Illustrations from Photographs, Old Prints and Pictures, Original Designs, Ornaments, etc. The book is planned as the first systematic and comprehensive guide to the simpler types of old furniture within the scope of the collector of average means. Med. 8vo. 12s. 6d. net.

OLD ENGLISH FURNITURE : THE OAK PERIOD, 1550-1630

Its Characteristics, Features, and Detail from Tudor Times to the Regency. For the use of Collectors, Designers, Students, and Others. By J. T. GARSIDE. Containing 30 Plates reproduced from the Author's specially prepared Drawings illustrating about 400 details of Table Legs; Bed-posts; Corbels; Friezes; Capitals; Panels; Inlay Motives; Metal Fittings, etc. Including also Drawings of type-pieces of the period and 20 Photographic Illustrations. With an Historical Introduction, etc. Cheaper reissue. 8vo, cloth, gilt. 7s. 6d. net.

FRENCH FURNITURE AND DECORATION OF THE LOUIS XIV AND REGENCY STYLES

A Pictorial review of their chief Types and Features in the Late XVIIth and early XVIIIth Centuries. By CORRADO RICCI. Comprising 414 Illustrations, mostly from Photographs of various types of Interiors, Galleries, Halls, with characteristic specimens of Chairs, Tables, Bureaux, Settees, Cabinets, Beds, Mirrors, Stools, etc. With brief Introductory Text, illustrated by reproductions of Designs, by Lepautre, Berain, Marot, Watteau and others. 4to, cloth, gilt. 38s. net.

OLD SILVER OF EUROPE AND AMERICA

From Early Times to the XIXth Century. By E. ALFRED JONES. A Survey of the Old Silver of England, America, Austria, Belgium, Canada, Czecho-Slovakia, Denmark, France, Germany, Holland, Hungary, Ireland, Italy, Norway, Poland, Portugal, Russia, Scotland, Spain, Sweden, Switzerland, etc. With a Chapter on Spurious Plate and 96 Photogravure Plates, comprising Illustrations of 537 subjects. Cheaper reissue. Crown 4to, art canvas, lettered in silver. 18s. net.

EIGHTEENTH-CENTURY ARCHITECTURE IN SOUTH AFRICA

By Professor G. E. PEARSE, F.R.I B.A., Witwatersrand University, Johannesburg. With 130 Collotype Plates, from Photographs and specially prepared Measured Drawings of Country and Town Buildings and their Features, showing Views, Elevations, Plans, Interiors, Carving, Gardens, etc. With full Text, illustrated by Sketches, Engravings, etc. *Large 4to, buckram, gilt. £2 10s. net. Edition strictly limited to 500 copies. The subscription price may be raised as the small number becomes nearly exhausted.*

THE FOUR VOLUMES OF

BATSFORD'S LIBRARY OF DECORATIVE ART

form an attractive Series of remarkable scope and completeness. It reviews the Development of English Decoration and Furniture during the three Renaissance Centuries, XVI, XVII, and XVIII (1500-1820). Each volume has an extensive series of Plates, and is a complete guide to the work of its Period. The volumes are remarkable for the beauty and number of their illustrations, the simplicity and clearness of their arrangement, and their moderate prices. The complete series is published at prices amounting to £10, but is supplied for the present at the special price of £9 net.

"These handsome volumes with their extremely fine and copious illustrations provide a full survey of English Furniture and Decoration."—*The Times.*

VOL. I. DECORATION AND FURNITURE IN ENGLAND DURING THE EARLY RENAISSANCE, 1500-1660

An Account of their Development and Characteristic Forms during the Tudor, Elizabethan and Jacobean Periods, by M. JOURDAIN. Containing about 300 pages, and over 200 full-page Plates (with Coloured Frontispiece and some in photogravure), including over 400 Illustrations, from specially made Photographs and Measured Drawings, and from Engravings. Folio (size 14 x 10½ in.), cloth, gilt. £2 10s. net.

VOL. II. FURNITURE IN ENGLAND FROM 1660 to 1760

By FRANCIS LENGYON. A Survey of the Development of its Chief Types. Containing 300 pages with over 400 Illustrations, from special Photographs, together with 5 in colour. Second Edition, revised with many new Illustrations. Folio (14 in. x 10½ in.), cloth, gilt. £2 10s. net.

VOL. III. DECORATION IN ENGLAND FROM 1640 to 1770

By FRANCIS LENGYON. A Review of its Development and Features. Containing 300 pages with over 350 Illustrations, of which 133 are full-page, from special Photographs, and 4 in colour. Second Edition, Revised and Enlarged. Folio (14 in. x 10½ in.), cloth, gilt. £2 10s. net.

VOL. IV. DECORATION AND FURNITURE IN ENGLAND DURING THE LATER XVIIITH CENTURY, 1760-1820

An Account of their Development and Characteristic Forms, by M. JOURDAIN. Containing about 300 pages, with over 180 full-page Plates (a selection in Collotype), including over 400 Illustrations, from specially made Photographs and Measured Drawings, and from Engravings. Folio (size 14 x 10½ in.), cloth, gilt. £2 10s. net.

HISTORIC INTERIORS IN COLOUR

Illustrated in a Series of 80 full-page Plates, reproduced in facsimile from Water-colours by well-known artists of Rooms of the later XVIIth to the early XIXth Centuries, in Baroque, Rococo, Louis XVI, and Empire Styles, in various Castles and private Houses in Germany, Austria, and France. Comprising Salons, Dining-rooms, Ante-rooms, Music Rooms, Cabinets, Bedrooms, Libraries, etc. With brief Text by A. Feulner. 4to, cloth, gilt. 40s. net.

A limited Edition of the first work on a fine, unknown Craft.

DOMESTIC UTENSILS OF WOOD

From the XVIth to the Mid-XIXth Century in England and on the Continent. By OWEN EVAN-THOMAS. Illustrated by 70 full-page Plates from specially arranged Photographs of 1000 subjects in the Author's personal collection. Including full Introductory, Historical and Descriptive Text. Large 4to, cloth, gilt. 21s. net.

THE LEVERHULME ART MONOGRAPHS

A Series of three sumptuous Volumes, folio, handsomely bound in art buckram, gilt. Price £15 15s. the set (volumes not sold separately). Edition strictly limited to 350 copies for sale, of which very few remain.

I. ENGLISH PAINTING OF THE XVIIIth AND XIXth CENTURIES

With some Examples of the Spanish, French, and Dutch Schools, and a Collection of Original Drawings and of Sculpture. By R. R. TATLOCK. Editor of the *Burlington Magazine*. With an Introduction by ROGER FRY. Containing 200 pages of Text, including Introductory Notes, and detailed Accounts of 1000 Pictures, Drawings, etc. Illustrated by 101 Photographic full-page Plates and 12 in Photogravure.

II. CHINESE PORCELAIN AND WEDGWOOD POTTERY

With other works of Ceramic Art. By R. L. HOBSON, B.A., British Museum. Containing 200 pages of Text, including Introductions and detailed descriptions of over 2000 Pieces. With over 75 Photographic Plates, and 30 Plates reproduced in colour.

III. ENGLISH FURNITURE, TAPESTRY, AND NEEDLEWORK OF THE XVIth-XIXth CENTURIES

With some Examples of Foreign Styles. By PERCY MACQUOID, R.I. Containing 150 pages of Text, with Introductions and detailed descriptions of over 700 Objects. Illustrated by 104 Photographic Plates, and 9 Plates in full colour.

The three fine volumes which the late Viscount Leverhulme planned as a memorial to his wife constitute a record of his own permanent collections. Only 350 sets can be offered for subscription, and the very moderate figure of £15 15s. represents but a fraction of the immense expenses undertaken by Viscount Leverhulme.

CHILDREN'S TOYS OF BYGONE DAYS

A History of Playthings of all Peoples from Prehistoric Times to the XIXth Century. By KARL GRÖBER. English Version by PHILIP HEREFORD. A beautifully produced survey, with a frontispiece and 11 Plates in colour, and 306 photographic illustrations of Dolls, Dolls-houses, Mechanical Toys, Carts, Ships, Tin Soldiers, etc., etc., of every country and period from the earliest times. With 66 pages of historical and descriptive text. 4to, canvas, gilt, with decorative wrapper. New and cheaper edition, 12s. 6d. net.

"Its abundance of illustrations is wonderful. Many of them are in colour, and all are reproduced in a fashion which does the publishers credit. The text is as interesting as the pictures. We can heartily recommend this book to the public. No one who buys it will be disappointed."—*The Daily Mail.*

An Attractive Account of a little-known XVIIIth Century Craftsman. Dedicated by gracious permission to Her Majesty Queen Mary.

JOHN OBRISSET

Huguenot, Carver, Medallist, Horn and Tortoise-shell Worker, and Snuff-box Maker. With examples of his Works dated 1705-1728. By PHILIP A. S. PHILLIPS. Containing Text on the Records of the Obrisset family, Writings on his Craftsmanship and Notes. With 104 Illustrations on 40 Plates, finely reproduced in Collotype, of Horn and Tortoise-shell Tobacco-boxes, Medals, Plaques in different Materials, Medallions, etc. Edition limited to 250 numbered copies, of which 210 are for sale. 4to, canvas, gilt, gilt top. £3 3s. net.

BATSFORD'S COLLECTORS' LIBRARY

A Series of Handbooks written by experts, providing information of practical value to Connoisseurs, Collectors, Designers, and Students. Each volume forms an ideal introduction to its subject, and is fully illustrated by Reproductions in Colour and from Photographs. The following volumes are still available. 8vo, cloth, gilt, price 6s. net each.

*OLD ENGLISH FURNITURE. By F. FENN and B. WYLLIE. With 94 Illustrations. *New Impression.*

OLD PEWTER. By MALCOLM BELL. With 106 Illustrations.

SHEFFIELD PLATE. By BERTIE WYLLIE. With 121 Illustrations.

FRENCH FURNITURE. By ANDRE SAGLIO. With 59 Illustrations.

DUTCH POTTERY AND PORCELAIN. By W. P. KNOWLES. With 54 Illustrations.

*PORCELAIN. By WILLIAM BURTON. With over 50 full-page Plates illustrating 87 fine examples of the Porcelain of Various Countries and Periods.

OLD PEWTER : ITS MAKERS AND MARKS

A Guide for Collectors, Connoisseurs, and Antiquaries. By HOWARD HERSCHEL COTTERELL, First Vice-President of the Society of Pewter Collectors. Containing about 500 pages, with 64 Plates of 200 Specimens of British Pewter, dated and described, and a List of 5000 to 6000 Pewterers, with Illustrations of their Touches and Secondary Marks, Facsimile Reproductions of existing Touch-Plates, and Text Illustrations. Cheaper reissue. Demy 4to, cloth, gilt. £3 3s. net.

"Messrs. Batsford's work as publishers is of their usual high standard, and Mr. Cotterell has enhanced his already great reputation as an authority, and is to be congratulated on this ideal standard work which will perforce be the last word on the subject for many years to come."—*The Queen.*

AN ILLUSTRATED HISTORY OF ENGLISH PLATE

Ecclesiastical and Secular, illustrating the Development of Silver and Gold Work of the British Isles from the earliest known examples to the latest of the Georgian Period. By Sir CHARLES JAMES JACKSON, F.S.A. With a Coloured Frontispiece, 76 Plates finely executed in Photogravure, and 1500 other Illustrations, chiefly from Photographs. Two volumes, small folio, bound in half-morocco. £10 10s. net.

A HISTORY OF ENGLISH WALLPAPER

From the earliest Period to 1914. By A. V. SUGDEN and J. L. EDMONDSON. Comprising 270 pages on Wallpapers' ancestry—Early Wallpapers—Eighteenth Century Developments—Famous Pioneers—Chinese Papers and English Imitations—Late Georgian Achievements—The Coming of Machinery—How Wallpaper "found itself"—The Coming of William Morris—Developments of Taste and Technique—Mill Records. With 70 Plates in colour and 190 Illustrations in half-tone. Large 4to. handsome art buckram, gilt, boxed. £3 3s. net.

OLD AND CURIOUS PLAYING CARDS

Their History and Types from many Countries and Periods. By H. T. MORLEY, B.Sc. (Arch.), F.R.Hist.S. With a Foreword by Sidney Lambert. Past-Master of the Company of Makers of Playing Cards. Containing Chapters on History, Asiatic, European and English Cards (including Caricature, Astrology, Heraldry, etc.), Musical Cards, Games, etc. With over 330 Illustrations, many in colour. Crown 4to, canvas, lettered, cloth sides. 21s. net; or handsomely bound in leather, 30s. net.

A HISTORY OF BRITISH WATER-COLOUR PAINTING

By H. M. Cundall, F.S.A. With a Foreword by Sir H. Hughes-Stanton, P.R.W.S. A New and Cheaper Edition, revised and enlarged, of this important standard work, with 64 full-page Illustrations in colour, and a full biographical list, arranged alphabetically, of the principal English Water-colourists. Large Medium 8vo, cloth, 15s. net.

"Apart from its value as a complete and authoritative work of reference in its specia subject the book forms a delightful picture gallery of the best British work in water-colours. The topographical and travel interest of the pictures reproduced has a wide range."—*Illustrated London News.*

THE BURLINGTON MAGAZINE MONOGRAPHS

Issued by the Publishers jointly with The Burlington Magazine

MONOGRAPH NO. I—CHINESE ART (*Out of print*)

MONOGRAPH NO. II—SPANISH ART

An Introductory Review of Architecture, Painting, Sculpture, Textiles, Ceramics, Woodwork, Metalwork, by Royall Tyler, Sir Charles Holmes and H. Isherwood Kay, Geoffrey Webb, A. F. Kendrick, B. Rackham and A. van de Put, Bernard Bevan, and P. de Artinano, respectively. With a General Introduction by R. R. Tatlock, Editor of *The Burlington Magazine.* Illustrated by 120 large scale reproductions of Paintings, Decorative Art, Buildings, etc., including 9 Plates in full colour, comprising 280 pictures in all. With Maps, Bibliography, etc. Royal 4to, cloth. Cheaper reissue, 25s. net.

MONOGRAPH NO. III—GEORGIAN ART

A Survey of Art in England during the reign of George III, 1760-1820, by leading authorities. The Sections comprise: *Painting* by J. B. Manson; *Architecture and Sculpture* by Geoffrey Webb; *Ceramics* by Bernard Rackham; *Woodwork* by Oliver Brackett; *Textiles* by A. F. Kendrick; *Minor Arts* by Louise Gordon-Stables. With an Introduction by Roger Fry. The Illustrations include 6 Plates in colour and 64 in half-tone, comprising some 100 subjects, and forming a gallery of the fine and decorative arts of the Period. Cheaper reissue. Royal 4to. cloth, 21s. net.

"This large volume gives an authoritative survey of the arts enumerated, and the quality of the reproductions maintains the high standard associated with its source. The high reputation of the associated authors and the beauty of the illustrations combine to render the book an ideal fulfilment of its purpose."—*Illustrated London News.*

THE DECORATIVE ARTS IN ENGLAND, 1660-1780

By H. H. Mulliner, with an Introduction by J. Starkie Gardner. A Series of 110 full-page Plates from Photographs illustrating 256 Specimens of Furniture, Lacquering, Marquetry, and Gesso, Chandeliers, Clocks; Stuart and Georgian Silver—Sconces, Cups, Bowls, Tea and Coffee Sets—Enamels, Locks, Battersea Enamel, Ormolu Vases, Tapestry, Needlework, Bookbindings. With brief Historical Introductions and full descriptions. Folio, half-parchment, gilt. £3 10s. net.

ENGLISH PLASTERWORK OF THE RENAISSANCE

A Review of its Design during the Period from 1500 to 1800. By M. Jourdain. Comprising over 100 full-page Plates of Elizabethan, Stuart, Georgian, and Adam ceilings, friezes, overmentels, panels, ornament, detail, etc., from specially taken Photographs and from Measured Drawings and Sketches. With an Illustrated Historical Survey on Foreign Influences and the Evolution of Design, Work and Names of Craftsmen, etc. New and cheaper reissue. Demy 4to, cloth. 15s. net.

THE EARLY FLEMISH PAINTINGS IN THE RENDERS COLLECTION

Exhibited at the Flemish Exhibition, Burlington House. With a full Introduction by G. HULIN DE LOO, and detailed Descriptions of the Paintings by E. MICHEL. Containing 6 Mounted Plates in full colour, and 18 Plates in Photogravure of Paintings in the Collection of M. Renders of Bruges, including works by Rogier van der Weyden, Memling, Jean Provost, Mabuse, the Masters of S. Veronica and of the Baroncelli Portraits, etc., etc. Large 4to, the few remaining copies offered in portfolio, £1 1s. net; or bound in cloth, gilt, £1 5s. net.

"With the book in his hands he would be a dull reader indeed who cannot in a comparatively short time familiarise himself with several distinct aspects of the history of Flemish painting."—*The Daily Telegraph.*

THE XVIIITH CENTURY IN LONDON

An Account of its Social Life and Arts. By E. BERESFORD CHANCELLOR. Containing 280 pages, with 192 Illustrations, printed in sepia, from Prints and Drawings by contemporary artists. With a Frontispiece in colour. Cheaper reissue. Crown 4to, cloth, gilt. 15s. net.

A Companion and Sequel to the above

LIFE IN REGENCY AND EARLY VICTORIAN TIMES

An Account of Social Life in the days of Brummel and D'Orsay. By E. BERESFORD CHANCELLOR. A Series of Chapters on the time of Brummel and D'Orsay, 1800-1843. With numerous Illustrations from Rare Prints and Original Drawings. Cheaper reissue. Large 8vo, cloth, gilt. 12s. 6d. net.

THE ART AND CRAFT OF GARDEN MAKING

By THOMAS H. MAWSON, assisted by E. PRENTICE MAWSON. Fifth Edition, Revised and Enlarged. Containing 440 pages, illustrated by 544 Plans, Sketches, and Photographs, and 5 colour Plates. Including Site, Entrances, Gates, Avenues, Terraces, Beds, Pergolas, Treillage, Rock and Water, Greenhouses, etc., etc., and list of Shrubs and Trees. Small folio, buckram, gilt. £3 15s. net.

GARDENS IN THE MAKING

By WALTER H. GODFREY. A simple Guide to the Planning of a Garden. With upwards of 70 Illustrations of Plans, Views, and various Garden Accessories. Crown 8vo, cloth. 7s. 6d. net.

SPANISH GARDENS

By Mrs. C. M. VILLIERS-STUART. A finely illustrated volume describing the beautiful and most famous gardens of Spain, by one of the foremost authorities on the subject. With 6 Plates in colour from the Author's original Water-colour Drawings, 80 pages of reproductions of gardens, statuary, cascades, garden features, etc., from Photographs, and numerous Illustrations in the text from old Engravings, Pen Drawings, etc. Small royal 8vo, cloth. 25s. net.

"All who love beautiful illustrated books and all who are interested in gardens will do well to buy this delightful volume. The plates in colours from the author's water-colour drawings are exquisite. This book is one of the most attractive we have seen."—*Daily Mail*

LITTLE KNOWN TOWNS OF SPAIN

A series of Water-colours and Drawings in facsimile colour and monochrome from the originals of VERNON HOWE BAILEY. Comprising 57 full-page Plates, many in colour, others in sepia, wash, lithography, etc., with text, including historical and descriptive short notes. Large 4to, in decorative paper binding, £1 10s. net.

ART IN THE LIFE OF MANKIND

A Survey of its Achievements from the Earliest Times. By ALLEN W. SEABY. Planned in a series of concise volumes, each containing about 80 pages of text ,with about 70 full-page and smaller Illustrations from the author's specially prepared Sketches and Drawings, and a series of 16 Photographic Plates. Crown 8vo, cloth, 5s. net per volume.

I. A GENERAL VIEW OF ART: ITS NATURE, MEANING, PRINCIPLES AND APPRECIATION. II. ANCIENT TIMES: THE ART OF ANCIENT EGYPT, CHALDÆA, ASSYRIA, PERSIA, and other lands. III. GREEK ART & ITS INFLUENCE. IV. ROMAN & BYZANTINE ART & THEIR INFLUENCE. Other volumes on Art.

These concise little volumes are designed to serve as an Introduction to the Appreciation and Study of Art in general. They are simply and graphically written and fully illustrated by many Drawings and Photographs.

A SHORT HISTORY OF ART

From Prehistoric times to the Nineteenth Century. Translated from the French of Dr. ANDRÉ BLUM. Edited and Revised by R. R. TATLOCK. Illustrated by 128 full-page Photographic Plates, comprising about 250 examples of the finest Painting, Sculpture, Architecture, and Decorative Art of Early, Classic, Byzantine, Gothic, Renaissance, and Recent Times. Including also about 100 Illustrations in the text from Drawings, Engravings, and Plans. Medium 8vo, cloth, gilt. 12s. 6d. net.

HISTORY OF ART

By JOSEPH PIJOAN, Professor at Pomona College, California. In 3 volumes, Royal 8vo, bound in cloth, gilt. 36s. net per volume (obtainable separately).

VOL. I. PRIMITIVE, ANCIENT AND CLASSIC ART. With 61 full-page Plates, including many in colour, and 876 Illustrations from Photographs, Plans, Drawings, Restorations, etc.

VOL. II. BYZANTINE, ISLAMIC, ROMANESQUE AND GOTHIC ART. With 52 double- and full-page Plates, including many in colour, and 856 Illustrations from Photographs, etc.

VOL. III. THE RENAISSANCE TO MODERN TIMES. With 34 full-page Plates, including many in colour and 776 Illustrations from Photographs, etc.

OLD MASTER DRAWINGS

A Quarterly Magazine, edited by K. T. PARKER, British Museum. With an Executive Committee of: CAMPBELL DODGSON, A. P. OPPÉ, M. HIND, and A. G. B. RUSSELL, and Consultative Foreign Authorities. Each number contains 16-20 Plates, and about 12 letterpress pages of articles and shorter notices dealing with Drawings from the earliest times to the 19th Century. Demy 4to. Annual subscription, 21s. net, post free; Single Numbers, 5s. 6d. net, post free.

No periodical devoted exclusively to the study and criticism of drawings has hitherto existed; this publication is intended to meet the need. The names of the many scholars connected with it guarantee its authoritative character, and its volumes are a mine of reference to students of art.

THE DRAWINGS OF ANTOINE WATTEAU, 1684-1721

By Dr. K. T. PARKER, of the British Museum, an Editor of "Old Master Drawings." A full, original and critical Survey. Illustrated by 100 Collotype Reproductions of selected characteristic Drawings from private and public collections, many unpublished, a Frontispiece in colour and 16 of the Master's most important pictures. With full, critical and descriptive letterpress. 4to, canvas cloth, gilt. £2 2s. net.

A MANUAL OF HISTORIC ORNAMENT

Being an Account of the Development of Architecture and the Historic Arts, for the use of Students and Craftsmen. By RICHARD GLAZIER, A.R.I.B.A. Fifth Edition, revised and enlarged. Containing 700 Illustrations, chiefly from the Author's Pen Drawings, including many new to this Edition from various sources, and a special series of Photographic Plates of Ornament of the Orient and the Renaissance. Large 8vo, cloth. 12s. 6d. net.

"The result of revision is admirable in every respect: the book is immensely improved, and its scope considerably broadened, though it is still compact and easy of reference. It is now the ideal manual for the student or craftsman, and those who are wise enough to purchase it will possess not only an invaluable work of reference, but a source of inspiration as well."—*The Decorator.*

A HANDBOOK OF ORNAMENT

With 3000 Illustrations of the Elements and the Application of Decoration to Objects, e.g., Vases, Frets, Diapers, Consoles, Frames, Jewellery, Heraldry, etc., grouped on over 300 Plates, reproduced from the Author's specially prepared Drawings. With descriptive text to each subject. By Professor F. SALES MEYER. Large 8vo, cloth, lettered. 16s. net.

"IT IS A LIBRARY, A MUSEUM, AN ENCYCLOPÆDIA, AND AN ART SCHOOL IN ONE. TO RIVAL IT AS A BOOK OF REFERENCE ONE MUST FILL A BOOKCASE. The quality of the drawings is unusually high, and the choice of examples is singularly good. . . . The text is well digested, and not merely descriptive or didactic, but an admirable mixture of example and precept. So good a book needs no praise."—*The Studio.*

THE STYLES OF ORNAMENT

From Prehistoric Times to the Middle of the XIXth Century. A Series of 3500 Examples Arranged in Historical Order, with descriptive text. By ALEXANDER SPELTZ. Revised and Edited by R. PHENÉ SPIERS, F.S.A., F.R.I.B.A. Containing 560 pages, with 400 full-page Plates exhibiting upwards of 3500 separate Illustrations. Large 8vo, cloth, gilt. 15s. net.

MR. WALTER CRANE, in a lengthy review in the *Manchester Guardian*, wrote: ". . . To pack into a single volume of some 626 pages and 400 illustrations a really intelligible account of the styles of ornament prevailing in the world from prehistoric times to the middle of the nineteenth century is A REMARKABLE FEAT. . . . The illustrations are for the most part well chosen and characteristic, and are drawn with decision and facility."

PATTERN DESIGN

For Students, treating in a practical way the Anatomy, Planning, and Evolution of Repeated Ornament. By LEWIS F. DAY. Containing about 300 pages, and 300 practical Illustrations from specially prepared Drawings and Photographs of the Principles of Repeat Design, the "Drop," the "Spot" Geometrical Ornament, etc. New edition, revised and enlarged by AMOR FENN, with many fresh Illustrations. Demy 8vo, cloth, gilt, 10s. 6d. net.

"Every line and every illustration in this book should be studied carefully and continually by every one having any aspiration toward designing."—*The Decorator.*

ABSTRACT DESIGN

A Practical Manual on the Making of Pattern. By AMOR FENN, late Head of the Art Section, Goldsmith's College, New Cross. A series of careful, informative sections on Conditions, Elements, etc. Illustrated by about 180 full-page Designs from the Author's specially-prepared Drawings. 8vo, cloth ,lettered. 12s. 6d. net.

ROUND THE WORLD IN FOLK TALES

A Regional Treatment. By RACHEL M. FLEMING. 16 Tales from Iceland, Mexico, Africa, Australia, etc., told in a fresh, easy style. With 17 Illustrations from Prints, Drawings, and Photographs. 8vo, boards, 2s. net. Cloth, 3s. net.

NATURE AND ORNAMENT

By LEWIS F. DAY. NATURE THE RAW MATERIAL OF DESIGN, treating chiefly of the decorative possibilities of Plant Form, its growth, features, and detail. With 350 Illustrations, chiefly grouped comparatively under Flowers, Seed Vessels, Fruits, Berries, etc., specially drawn by Miss J. FOORD. New Edition, revised, with a Chapter by MARY HOGARTH. Demy 8vo, cloth, lettered. 7s. 6d. net.

FLORAL FORMS IN HISTORIC DESIGN

Drawn by LINDSAY P. BUTTERFIELD, Designer, with Introduction and Notes by W. G. PAULSON TOWNSEND. Containing 30 Plates in Collotype and Line, showing about 100 Decorative Adaptations of the Rose, Carnation, Fruit Blossom, etc., from Eastern and European stuffs, and from old Herbals. Large folio, in portfolio. 15s. net.

MODERN DECORATIVE ART IN ENGLAND

A Series of Illustrations of its Development and Characteristics, with Introductory Text by W. G. PAULSON TOWNSEND. Cheaper reissue. Large 4to, cloth, gilt. 12s. 6d. net.

TEXTILES, PRINTED FABRICS, WALL PAPERS, LACE AND EMBROIDERY, TAPESTRY, STENCILLING, BATIK, etc. Illustrating on 80 Plates 178 examples, including 51 subjects beautifully reproduced in full colour.

THE PRACTICAL DRAWING SERIES

DRAWING FOR ART STUDENTS AND ILLUSTRATORS

By ALLEN W. SEABY. Containing 220 pages, with 113 Illustrations printed in Sepia, mostly full page Plates, from Drawings by Old and Modern Artists. Second Edition, revised and enlarged. Medium 8vo, cloth, paper sides. 10s. 6d. net.

COMPOSITION

An Analysis of the Principles of Pictorial Design. By CYRIL C. PEARCE, R.B.A. With chapters on Tone, Distribution, Gradation, Scale, Perspective, Rhythm, Harmony and Balance of Colour, Discords. Illustrated by 130 comparative and analytical Drawings, Sketches, and Diagrams, 6 Plates in colour, and 28 full-page Illustrations from Paintings by great Masters. Medium 8vo, cloth, gilt, paper sides. 10s. 6d. net.

PEN DRAWING

A Practical Manual on Materials, Technique, Style, Texture, etc. By G. M. ELLWOOD. Containing sections on History—Technique—Materials—Figures, Faces and Hands—Style and Methods—Landscape and Architecture—Modern Work—Magazine Illustration—Humorous Drawing Advertisements—Fashion. With numerous practical Diagrams by the Author, and 100 pages of Illustrations by the chief Pen Draughtsmen of present and recent times. Medium 8vo, cloth, gilt, paper sides. 10s. 6d. net.

THE ART OF DRAWING IN LEAD PENCIL

By JASPER SALWEY, A.R.I.B.A. A Practical Manual dealing with Materials, Technique, Notes and Sketching, Building up, Form and Style, Process Reproduction, etc. Second Edition, revised and enlarged. Containing 232 pages with 122 finely printed reproductions of selected Pencil Drawings of Land and Seascapes. Figure-Studies, Book-Illustrations, etc. Medium 8vo, cloth, gilt, paper sides. 10s. 6d. net.

THE PRACTICAL DRAWING SERIES—(continued)

THE ART AND PRACTICE OF SKETCHING

A Comprehensive Treatise on the Practice of Sketching by every method. By JASPER SALWEY, A.R.I.B.A. The Author deals successively with varous media—Pen, Pencil, Water-colour, Oil, Wash, Crayon, Chalk, etc., and gives a complete account of the Technique of each. Illustrated by 64 Plates of half-tone illustration and 6 Plates in colour, with various Line Illustrations in the text from the work of great Masters. Medium 8vo, cloth, paper sides. 10s. 6d. net.

SKETCHING IN LEAD PENCIL

By JASPER SALWEY, A.R.I.B.A. An Introduction to the same author's "Art of Drawing in Lead Pencil," but dealing entirely with sketching as differentiated from the making of finished Drawings. A practical manual for the Architect, Student and Artist. Containing 111 pages and 56 Illustrations, by well-known artists in the medium, and by the author. Medium 8vo, cloth, gilt, paper sides. 7s. 6d. net.

ANIMAL ANATOMY AND DRAWING

By EDWIN NOBLE. Illustrated by a series of Plates in facsimile of the Author's Drawings of HORSES, CATTLE, DOGS, BIRDS, AND WILD ANIMALS, representing also Features, Details, etc. Including also numerous full-page and smaller Line Drawings of Anatomy, Muscles, Bones, etc. Medium 8vo, cloth, gilt, paper sides. 10s. 6d. net.

SKETCHING FROM NATURE

A Practical Treatise on the Principles of Pictorial Composition. By F. J. GLASS. CONTENTS: Choice of Subject and Planning of Sketch—Tones—Exercises in Composition—Examples from the Old Masters. With 6 Plates in colour and numerous composition from the Author's Drawings, and a series of Plates by Peter de Wint, Crome, Constable, Harpignies, Bonington, etc. Medium 8vo, cloth. 10s. 6d. net.

FASHION DRAWING AND DESIGN

By LOUIE E. CHADWICK. Illustrated by numerous examples of Historic Fashion Plates, Explanatory Sketches by the Author, Figure Studies, and a series of about 80 full-page and double Plates of Contemporary Fashion Drawings by well-known artists. Cheaper reissue. Large 8vo, cloth, lettered. 7s. 6d. net.

COLOUR: A MANUAL OF ITS STUDY AND PRACTICE

By H. BARRETT CARPENTER, late Headmaster of the School of Art, Rochdale. A Series of 16 concise but very practical chapters, based on the Author's experiments, on Harmony—Contrast—Discord—Keynotes—Intermingling—Effect of Lighting—Dirty Colour—Black-and-White, etc. Illustrated by 24 Plates (some double size), printed in colour; giving 40 Examples of Colour Combinations, Grading, Toning, etc., including some new examples of application in Historic Design. New and Revised Impression. 8vo, cloth, gilt. 9s. net.

"This book has been revised and enlarged, making it a treasure for all who wish to understand the value of colour. Like most of the books published by this house, the type is bold and clear and the many coloured illustrations are really beautiful. I feel this book will bring sunshine into the darkest day, and would recommend it to all."—*Arts and Crafts Journal.*

A COLOUR CHART

Issued in connection with the above book. Consisting of a circle 17 inches in diameter, printed in Graded Colour, showing 14 shades, Combinations and Contrasts. With explanatory letterpress. Folio, stout paper. 2s. 6d. net.

ART IN DAILY LIFE FOR YOUNG AND OLD

By D. D. SAWER. A comprehensive practical course for Teachers, Students, and Art Lovers; treating of the Place of Drawing, Plants and their Use, Figure Drawing and Drapery, Animal Drawing, Modelling Shapes and Figures, Casting, Clay Modelling, Object Drawing, Notes on Crafts, Composition, Design, applied and graphic. Each chapter is divided into three sections: A historical résumé, a note on educational significance and a briefer review of its practice and technique. With 10 Plates in Colour, and numerous full-page and text Illustrations in Line and Half-tone. Medium 8vo, cloth, lettered. 12s. 6d. net.

EVERYDAY ART AT SCHOOL AND HOME

By D. D. SAWER. A Practical Course based on the new Board of Education "Suggestions to Teachers," and adaptable to Dalton Methods, containing graduated lessons on Brushwork, Design, Flower-painting, etc., with sections on Architectural Drawing, Lettering, Stained Glass, Leather-work, and other Crafts. With 64 Plates in half-tone, from the Author's Drawings, numerous full-page and smaller Line Illustrations, and 8 Plates in colour, many Verse Extracts, etc. Medium 8vo, cloth. 12s. 6d. net.

PERSPECTIVE IN DRAWING

A simple Introductory Account. By Miss D. D. SAWER, late Art Lecturer at the Diocesan College, Brighton, Author of "Everyday Art at School and Home." With an Introduction by Professor ALLEN W. SEABY, Headmaster, School of Art, University of Reading. With Sections on Basic Principles, the Cube, Cylinder, Shadows, Reflections, Aerial Perspective, Colour, and Drawing. Illustrated by over 100 Diagrams and Sketches, a Frontispiece in colour, specially drawn by the Author, and reproductions from Photographs. Crown 8vo, cloth, 5s. net.

SKETCHING AND PAINTING FOR YOUNG AND OLD

An Elementary Practical Manual, by D. D. SAWER, late Art Mistress, Brighton Diocesan Training College, Author of "Everyday Art Perspective," etc. With chapters on: Ungathered Wealth, a Day Out, Materials, Practice, the First Sketch Out of Doors, Composition, Mounting and Framing. Illustrated by coloured Frontispiece, 8 Plates in Line and half-tone, and 31 text Illustrations from the Author's specially prepared Sketches, Diagrams, etc. Crown 8vo, stiff covers, 1s. 6d. net; or quarter-cloth, lettered, 2s. net.

THE ART OF THE BODY

Rhythmic Exercises for Health and Beauty. By MARGUERITE AGNIEL, Dancer and Physical Instructress. A series of simple, easy and enjoyable exercises, illustrated by numerous Photographic Plates, specially posed by the Author. With 100 subjects on 64 Plates, including many reproductions of dance poses and figure studies, draped and nude. CONTENTS: Function of the Spine—How to Walk Well—Figure Reducing—Exercises for the Digestive Organs, Back and Neck—Legs and Ankles—The Care of the Hands and Feet—Skin, Eyes and Teeth—Constipation—Women's Disorders, etc. Cheaper reissue. Large 8vo, cloth, gilt. 12s. 6d. net.

"For some years past I have been much interested in the ideas which Miss Marguerite Agniel not only advocates but so skilfully and delightfully embodies. By her own personal experiences she has been especially fitted to demonstrate the harmonious union of the æsthetic and hygienic aspects of physical exercise. There must be many to whom her work will prove fascinating and valuable."—HAVELOCK ELLIS

THE HUMAN FORM AND ITS USE IN ART

A Series of 118 Photographic Studies on 73 Plates from specially selected Female and Child Models, by F. R. YERBURY, including a Series of Male Studies by F. H. CROSSLEY, F.S.A. With an Introduction by G. M. ELLWOOD. Illustrated by 17 Photographic Plates and numerous Text Figures. With descriptive Notes on the Poses. Large 8vo, cloth. 18s. net.

LIVING SCULPTURE

A Record of Expression in the Human Figure by BERTRAM PARK and YVONNE GREGORY. With an historical and descriptive Introduction by G. MONTAGUE ELLWOOD. Comprising a Series of 47 full-page Studies of Selected Male and Female Figures with descriptive Notes. The Introduction is illustrated by 9 plates, giving 16 examples of the Human Form in Prehistoric, Greek, Renaissance and newest Art. Cheaper reissue. Small 4to, cloth, gilt. 12s. 6d. net.

LAUGHS AND SMILES and How to Draw Them. By A. A. BRAUN.

Containing 45 Plates, printed in tints of numerous constructional sketches, building up in successive stages humorous likenesses of well-known personages, and also figures from old Masters. Comprising in all about 300 Sketches by the Author, with concise instructive Text, including numerous anatomical Diagrams. Oblong 4to, decorative boards, cloth back. 3s. 6d. net.

"A book which young art students, or anyone with a practical taste for art, would appreciate. This attractive manual on humorous portrait-drawing should have a wide appeal."—*Overseas Daily Mail.*

FIGURES, FACES AND FOLDS

A Reference Book on Costume and the Female Countenance and Form. For Fashion Artists, Dress Designers, and Art Students. By ADOLPHE ARMAND BRAUN. Containing 112 comparative Plates, giving over 300 Illustrations of Costume and Drapery, and of typical Women's Faces, from antique statues and paintings. Including a special series of nude and draped studies from selected models specially posed for fashion work. With practical text, Dress diagrams, Figure details, Anatomy analysis, etc. Cheaper reissue. Demy 4to, stiff paper covers, 10s. 6d. net; cloth, gilt, 12s. 6d. net.

THE CHILD IN ART AND NATURE

By A. A. BRAUN. Containing chapters on Anatomy, Development, and Expression, and over 300 Illustrations from Photographs and Drawings of child poses, expressions, the Child Figure in Art. Second Edition, revised and enlarged. Cheaper reissue. 4to, in stiff covers, 10s. 6d. net; or cloth, gilt, 12s. 6d. net.

ALPHABETS, OLD AND NEW

With 224 complete Alphabets, 30 series of Numerals, many Ancient Dates, etc. Selected and Arranged by LEWIS F. DAY. With a short account of the Development of the Alphabet. Crown 8vo, cloth. 5s. net.

"A book which has, perhaps, proved more helpful than any ever before issued on the subject of alphabets."—*The Decorator.*

A valuable and attractive little Manual.

PEN PRACTICE

By WALTER HIGGINS. Chapters on Tools, Broad-pen Practice, Spacing, Italics, Uncials and Half-uncials, Setting out, A Cursive Hand, etc. With 27 Plates specially drawn by the Author, giving some hundreds of Letters, Ornaments and Exercises, and 6 from selected Historical Examples. Crown 8vo, stiff paper covers, 1s. 6d. net; or cloth, lettered, 2s. 6d. net.

THE ROMAN ALPHABET AND ITS DERIVATIVES

A large-sized Reproduction of the Alphabet of the Trajan Column. By ALLEN W. SEABY. A Series of large Plates, printed from the wood blocks, and including typical examples of Renaissance, Gothic, and Modern Alphabets and Types. With Introduction and descriptive Notes. Medium 4to, half-bound, lettered, or in portfolio. 4s. 6d. net.

DRAWING, DESIGN AND CRAFTWORK

For Teachers, Students, and Designers. By FREDK. J. GLASS. Containing 224 pages, with over 1750 Illustrations on 214 Plates, from Drawings by the Author. Third Edition, revised and enlarged with many new Plates. Demy 8vo, cloth. 12s. net.

MODELLING

A Practical Treatise for the Use of Students, etc. By F. J. GLASS. Containing Chapters on Modelling for Bronze, Wood, Stone, Terra-Cotta, etc; Modelling a Bust from Life; Figure Modelling; Relief Work; Composition; Casting; Gelatine Moulding; Proportionate Enlargement, etc. With an additional section on the History of Sculpture and Modelled Ornament. Illustrated by about 30 Plates of comparative stages and processes of Modelling, with about 35 Plates of the greatest Sculpture of all Periods, together with many Line Illustrations in the text. Royal 8vo, cloth, gilt. 15s. net.

ETCHING CRAFT

An Illustrated Guide for Students and Collectors. By W. P. ROBINS, R.E. With a Foreword by MARTIN HARDIE, Victoria and Albert Museum. Containing 250 pages on History, Technique, the work of the great Etchers, Dry-point, Aquatint, etc. Illustrated by 100 Plates of Etchings by Dürer, Rembrandt, Hollar, Whistler, Brangwyn, Clausen, Augustus John, Meryon, Forain, Zorn, and many other famous Etchers. Large 8vo, half-bound, gilt. 10s. 6d. net (formerly 21s. net).

PRACTICAL WOODCARVING

By ELEANOR ROWE. Third Edition, revised and enlarged, in Two Parts: I. ELEMENTARY WOODCARVING, embodying "Hints on Woodcarving." With numerous Illustrations, many full-page, from Drawings and Photographs of carving operations, examples and details. II. ADVANCED WOODCARVING. With numerous Illustrations, many full-page, from Drawings and Photographs of historic and modern carvings. Demy 8vo, limp cloth, lettered. 5s. net each; or two parts in one volume, cloth, gilt, 10s. net

ONE HUNDRED AND ONE THINGS FOR A BOY TO MAKE

By A. C. HORTH. With Notes on Workshop Practice and Processes, Tools, Joints, and full reliable directions for making Working Models. Illustrated by numerous full-page and smaller practical Diagrams and Sketches specially prepared. Second Edition, revised and enlarged. Crown 8vo, cloth. 5s. net.

DINNER BUILDING

A Book of entertaining and practical instruction in the Noble Arts of Cooking and Eating. Written by W. TEIGNMOUTH SHORE. With an Introduction by GILBERT FRANKAU. A series of 42 bright, stimulating but practical Talks on such subjects as The Perfect Dinner, Sandwichery, Remnant Days, Cabbages and Things, incorporating hundreds of fresh recipes of all kinds. Cheaper reissue. F'cap 8vo, cloth, lettered. 2s. net.

SAMPLERS AND STITCHES

A Handbook of the Embroiderer's Art. By MRS. ARCHIBALD CHRISTIE. Containing 34 full-page Reproductions from Photographs, a Frontispiece in colour, and 239 Text Drawings. Second Edition, revised and enlarged. Crown 4to, boards, canvas back. 25s. net.

ART IN NEEDLEWORK

A Book about Embroidery. By Lewis F. Day and Mary Buckle. Fourth Edition, revised by Mary Hogarth. Including a specially worked Series of Stitch-Samplers, numerous supplementary Diagrams and many Plates of Historic Embroidery—Chinese, Mediæval, Italian, French, and Modern English. With additional Examples of Modern Work by Duncan Grant, Mrs. Newall, Mrs. Stoll, D. Hager, and others. Containing 280 pages, 80 full-page Plates, reproduced from Photographs, and 50 Illustrations in the text. Crown 8vo, cloth. 7s. 6d. net.

SIMPLE STITCH PATTERNS FOR EMBROIDERY

By Anne Brandon-Jones. With coloured Frontispiece and 13 Photographic Plates illustrating 44 Patterns, 4 Plates from the Author's Pen Drawings, showing 31 Stitch Diagrams and 11 Complete Objects. With an Introduction, Chapters on the Method, Sketches, Colour Materials and Application of Designs, also descriptive Notes, with Colour Schemes. Crown 4to, paper wrappers, 2s. 6d. net; or in cloth, 3s. 6d.

"There is valuable help in this book. There are excellent plates in line and colour. The directions are clear and concise, and the articles suggested for practice are such as will please young people to make."—*Education Outlook.*

STITCH PATTERNS AND DESIGNS FOR EMBROIDERY

By Anne Brandon-Jones. An independent companion volume to the above work, containing 48 pages with 45 photographic examples on 12 Plates of simple and effective embroidery Motives, a Frontispiece in colour, and numerous Text Illustrations of Stitches and Methods. Crown 4to, paper wrappers, 3s. od. net; or in cloth, 4s. od. net.

CANVAS EMBROIDERY

A Manual for Students and Amateurs by Louisa F. Pesel. Containing 48 pages of text, a coloured Frontispiece, and 14 specially prepared Plates showing Stitches and methods. Medium oblong 4to, paper wrappers, 3s. net; or bound in cloth, 4s. net.

ENGLISH EMBROIDERY. I. DOUBLE-RUNNING, or BACK STITCH

By Louisa F. Pesel. With coloured Frontispiece, 10 specially drawn Plates of 45 Working Designs, and 8 Plates from Photographs of 10 English and Coptic Samplers, comprising numerous Patterns and Motives. With Practical Text and a Preface by Etta Campbell, Embroidery Teacher, Winchester School of Arts. Uniform with "Canvas Embroidery." Large oblong 4to, paper wrappers, 3s. net; or boards, cloth back, 4s. net.

ENGLISH EMBROIDERY. II. CROSS-STITCH

By Louisa F. Pesel. With a Coloured Frontispiece, 10 specially drawn Plates of 32 Working Designs, etc., and 8 Plates from Photographs of 15 typical English Samplers and Objects. Comprising 43 subjects, giving hundreds of Patterns and Motives. With Practical Text and a Preface by Professor R. Gleadowe, late Slade Professor of Fine Arts, Oxford University. Large oblong 4to, paper wrappers, 3s. net; or boards, cloth back, 4s. net.

HISTORIC TEXTILE FABRICS

By Richard Glazier. Containing: Materials—The Loom—Pattern—Tapestries—Dyed and Printed Fabrics—Church Vestments, etc., with about 100 Plates from Photographs and from the Author's Drawings, including 4 in colour, and 43 Line Diagrams, illustrating over 200 varieties of Textile Design. Large 8vo, cloth, gilt. 21s. net.

ILLUSTRATED STITCHERY DECORATIONS

By Winifred M. Clarke. Containing 19 Plates from the Author's specially prepared Drawings, giving some 120 useful original Motives: Borders, Rosettes, Floral Elements, Patterns, Lettering and Worked Objects, such as Bags, Blotters, etc. Including a coloured Frontispiece, Introductory Text and full descriptive Notes on the Plates. Crown 4to, stiff paper wrappers, 3s. net; boards, cloth back, 4s. net.

"A new and extremely useful little book for the embroidery worker. Miss Clarke has succeeded admirably in her task."—*Edinburgh Evening News.*

THE BOOK OF WEAVING

By Anna Nott Shook, U.S.A. Containing 190 pages, with 12 Plates in colour, comprising 34 Examples, and 31 Plates of about 130 Drawings, many in half-tone. Small 4to, cloth, lettered. 15s. net.

The aim of this work is to make the use of the handloom practicable and profitable in homes, schools, and institutions. The text is in 5 sections, on Weaving To-day and Yesterday, How to Weave, What to Weave, Art in Weaving (Design, Colour, Dyeing), Who Should Weave; with full information on equipment, processes and materials. The drawings show details of working and suggested designs, and the examples in colour are from pieces woven by the Author's pupils, such as tapestry, rugs, bags, cushion covers, shawls, scarves, etc.

THE ART AND CRAFT OF OLD LACE

In all Countries, from the XVIth to the Early XIXth Centuries. By Alfred von Henneberg. With an Introduction by Wilhelm Pinder. Containing a full original account of the Development of Style and an Analysis of Technique and Texture. Including descriptive Notes and a Bibliography. Illustrated by 190 full-page Plates, 8 in colour, giving 60 specimens from scale diagrams and 250 of the finest pieces of Old Lace. Large 4to, cloth, gilt. £3 3s. net.

THE SMALLER HOUSE OF TO-DAY

By Gordon Allen, F.R.I.B.A., Winner of the *Daily Mail* Prize for the Best £1500 House. Containing Notes on Sites and Subsoils, Plans, Exteriors, Methods, Interiors, Hygiene, Gardens, Finance, etc. With 2 Plates in colour, 64 from Photographs, and 153 Illustrations from Line Drawings of Houses, Plans, and Designs. Medium 8vo, cloth. 10s. 6d. net.

THE CHEAP COTTAGE AND SMALL HOUSE

By J. Gordon Allen, F.R.I.B.A. New Edition, remodelled and enlarged, containing over 150 Illustrations from Drawings and Photographs of Cottages and their Plans, Housing Schemes, etc., from the latest Designs. Medium 8vo, cloth. 8s. 6d. net.

THE ART AND CRAFT OF HOME MAKING

A Comprehensive Guide with an Appendix of Household Recipes. By Edward W. Gregory. Second Edition, revised, with additional Chapters and new Illustrations. Containing Practical Hints and Information on such subjects as Taking a House—Wallpapers—Furnishing Various Rooms — Pictures — Kitchen — Heating — Carpets — Curtains — Things that Get Out of Order—Costs, etc. Containing 224 pages, with 9 Plates in full colour of decorative schemes by Gordon Blunt, numerous Photographs of Interiors by well-known architects, and many Sketches, Plans, and Diagrams in the text. Square 8vo, cloth lettered. 7s. 6d. net.

A BOOK OF BUNGALOWS AND MODERN HOMES

A series of Typical Designs and Plans. By CECIL J. H. KEELEY, F.S.I., A.R.San.I., Architect. Comprising 36 Designs, with large scale Plans, Brief Descriptions and Estimated Cost, including some Two-Storey Houses, Frontispiece in colour, Interior Views, Photographic Plates, etc. Large 8vo, cloth, lettered. 7s. 6d. net.

"The work may be recommended to those people who are on the look-out for homes designed with intelligence and convenience, and who have an eye for charm and artistic finish."—*Field.*

ARCHITECTURAL DRAWING, PERSPECTIVE AND RENDERING

By CYRIL A. FAREY, A.R.I.B.A., and A. TRYSTAN EDWARDS, A.R.I.B.A. Containing accounts of Measured Work Colouring, Sketching, Methods of Technique, Shading, Competition Drawings, Publicity and Posters, etc. Including a specially prepared Perspective in various stages by C. A. FAREY and Drawings by William Walcot, R.A., F. Brangwyn, R.A., W. Curtis Green, A.R.A., P. D. Hepworth, J. D. M. Harvey, and other well-known draughtsmen. With 43 Plates in half-tone, 9 in colour, 31 Line Reproductions, and 196 pages of Text. Cr. 4to, cloth. 16s. net.

ARCHITECTURAL DRAWING

By G. GORDON HAKE, F.R.I.B.A., and E. H. BUTTON, Architects. An Introductory Treatise for Architects and Students on Architectural Drawing of every type and in every medium. With 96 pages of text, 16 pages of Half-tone Illustrations and about 90 Line Illustrations in the text. Cheaper reissue. Medium 8vo, cloth. 7s. 6d. net.

"An excellent little book which every student should possess. The illustrations are uniformly good, and the general turn-out is of the high quality we expect from Batsford's." —*Illustrated Carpenter and Builder.*

FURNITURE FOR SMALL HOUSES

A Series of Designs. By PERCY A. WELLS. Containing 56 Plates reproduced from Photographs and Working Drawings by the Author, together with Illustrations in the text. Cheaper reissue. Small 4to, cloth. 7s. 6d. net.

"Mr. Wells's main concern is with the practical needs of a small house, and from this point of view his work is quite excellent. The photographs maintain the high standard which we associate with Messrs. Batsford's publications and the book should be read and studied by all who are interested in the long-awaited renascence of English cabinet-making."—*The Athenæum.*

HANDCRAFT IN WOOD AND METAL

A Handbook for the use of Teachers, Students, Craftsmen, and others. By JOHN HOOPER and ALFRED J. SHIRLEY. With over 300 Illustrations from Drawings and Photographs. Second Edition, revised and enlarged. Large 8vo, cloth, lettered. 10s. 6d. net.

CRAFTWORK IN METAL

A Practical Elementary Textbook for Teachers, Students, and Workers. By ALFRED J. SHIRLEY. Comprising a series of progressive Lessons and Exercises, illustrated by numerous full-page Plates from the Author's Drawings, each accompanied by detailed working directions, including also Practical Notes, Tables, etc. Medium 8vo, cloth. 5s. net.

"It bears the imprint of the successful practical teacher—hence its value to other teachers of the craft. We predict the book will be extensively used by teachers and students in the metalwork centres."—*The London Schoolmaster.*

SHOULD WE STOP TEACHING ART?

By C. R. ASHBEE. An interesting and outspoken account of modern Art Education. 8vo, boards, buckram back. 3s. 6d. net.

THE NEW MOVEMENT IN THE THEATRE

By LEON MOUSSINAC. With a Foreword by GORDON CRAIG. An elaborate International Survey of the Characteristics and Development of the Theatre in post-war Europe and America. With 120 Collotype Plates, comprising 250 figures and Costume Studies of which 115 are in colour. Also 235 Stage Settings, etc., many of them in colour. Introductory text translated and adapted by R. H. Packman. Thick Folio, buckram, gilt, £10 10s. net.

"I cannot praise this magnificent book too much. Its bountiful illustrations are the only way in which the stage developments of the last ten years could be conveyed. There can be no one who is connected with the theatre who would not get instruction and enjoyment from it."—*New Statesman.*

THE NEW STYLE

Architecture and Design. A Survey of its First Phase in Europe and America. With an Introduction adapted from the French of MAURICE CASTEELS, and descriptive notes on the Plates. Comprising 144 full-page Plates in Photogravure of Buildings, Interiors, Furniture, Lighting, etc., by well-known modern architects such as Le Corbusier, Mendelsohn, Gropius, Dudock, Mallet-Stevens, etc., chosen to illustrate the new movement in all its most representative manifestations. 4to, cloth, gilt. 12s. 6d. net.

THE NEW INTERIOR DECORATION

An Introduction to its Principles and International Survey of its Methods. By DOROTHY TODD and RATMOND MORTIMER. With over 200 Illustrations on 96 Plates of Interiors of every sort, Furniture, Carpets, Textiles, Lighting, Wall Painting, etc., of the new school by such Architects and Artists as Le Corbusier, Mallet-Stevens, Gropius, Oud, Duncan Grant, Lescaze, etc. With a frontispiece in colour from a drawing by E. MCKNIGHT KAUFFER and full Introductory and Practical Text. Demy 4to, art canvas, with decorative wrapper by E. MCKNIGHT KAUFFER. 12s. 6d. net.

MODERN THEATRES AND CINEMAS

By P. MORTON SHAND. A series of 80 plates giving over 100 examples of exteriors, interiors, foyers, vestibules, lighting, mural decoration, details, etc., of Theatres and Cinemas in the modern post-war style in France, Germany, England, Scandinavia, Italy, America, etc. Containing reproductions of the work of such architects as Margold, Kaufmann, Siclis, Gropius, Lipp, Ionides, Sauvage, de Soissons, Wilms, Mendelsohn, etc. Containing in addition numerous plans, elevations, sections in the text. Large 8vo, art canvas. 15s. net.

"A most interesting book; its illustrations are superb. You don't need to be an architect to enjoy reading this book. All you need is an intellectual curiosity into what is being done in the world to evolve new architectural forms. It is not only intensely interesting to read but it teaches you also what is going on in other countries."—*Tatler.*

REPRESENTATIVE BRITISH ARCHITECTS OF THE PRESENT DAY

By PROFESSOR C. H. REILLY, M.A., F.R.I.B.A., Director of the Liverpool School of Architecture, Author of "Recent Street Architecture," etc. An Account of Twelve Typical Distinguished Figures, their Careers and Work, including Professor Adshead, Robert Atkinson, Sir Herbert Baker, Sir R. Blomfield, A. J. Davis, E. Guy Dawber, Clough Williams-Ellis W. Curtis Green, H. V. Lanchester, Sir E. L. Lutyens, Sir Giles Gilbert Scott, and Walter Tapper. Illustrated by 80 Photographic Plates, including 12 Portraits, and Exterior and Interior Views of well-known Buildings. Large 8vo, cloth, gilt, 7s. 6d. net.

INDEX OF AUTHORS' NAMES

Made and Printed in Great Britain by The Stanhope Press Ltd, Rochester

Keep simple good colour
Prepare Canvas etc etc.